Opening up
John's Gospel

ANDREW PATERSON

DayOne

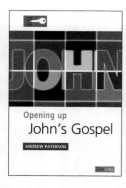

Opening up
John's Gospel

ANDREW PATERSON

Opening up John's Gospel is a brilliant, concise guide to John's Gospel. It helps the reader to understand John's profound revelation of Jesus the divine Messiah by vividly bringing to life the Jewish world of the first century and explaining the Old Testament background to so much of Jesus's teaching. It ably guides the reader through the narrative structure of the Gospel so that its overall message is grasped, rather than just favourite texts being appreciated. Many contemporary illustrations and practical applications help the reader to respond rightly to Jesus today. The questions for further study at the end of each chapter are really helpful and will enable readers to think more deeply for themselves. Although this book is short, the author has clearly drawn deeply on the very best biblical scholarship and makes judicious judgements when interpreting difficult or disputed passages. This book will inspire any Christian reader to know, love, worship and obey Jesus better, and there are many ideas to stimulate preachers. It would also be suitable for serious inquirers who are interested in finding out more about Jesus. All in all, an excellent book.

John Stevens, Director, Fellowship of Independent Evangelical Churches (FIEC), UK

John's Gospel—how easy to miss the wood for the trees! But this excellent study guide will help you identify both. A terrific resource for personal and group Bible study. Highly recommended!

Steve Brady, Principal, Moorlands Bible College, Christchurch, UK

Highly accessible and exceptionally practical.

Jonathan Stephen, Principal, Wales Evangelical School of Theology, UK

A reliable, accessible, and practical guide to this wonderful gospel.

Christopher Ash, Director, Cornhill Training Course, UK

Like an experienced tour guide leading us through a foreign country, Andrew Paterson takes us on an illuminating journey through John's Gospel. If you have ever felt daunted by John's Gospel, this little commentary will soon help you to feel at home. It strikes just the right balance between drawing our attention to the details of the text and showing us how those details fit together, so that we feel that we are travelling down the main road of John's message. Above all, I was struck by how some of the moments in Jesus's ministry that are well known but not always very well understood are made wonderfully clear and vivid by the way Andrew opens up the Old Testament background to what Jesus was doing. I can't wait to get people at church using this book to help them with their personal study or daily devotions—it will open up John's Gospel to them. But more than that, it will open their hearts to the Jesus of John's Gospel, and give them strength to go on believing that he is 'the Christ, the Son of God, and that by believing [they] may have life in his name' (John 20:31).

Mike Cain, Emmanuel Church, Bristol, UK

ISBN 978-1-84625-194-8

British Library Cataloguing in Publication Data available

Published by Day One Publications

Ryelands Road, Leominster, England, HR6 8NZ

Telephone 01568 613 740   FAX 01568 611 473

email—sales@dayone.co.uk

web site—www.dayone.co.uk

North American e-mail—usasales@dayone.co.uk

North American web site—www.dayonebookstore.com

Printed by Thomson Litho, East Kilbride

To Becca and Joe
'Look, the Lamb of God, who
takes away the sin of the world!'

Acknowledgements

The words in this book bear little resemblance to a preaching series in John that ran for over four years in the life of Kensington Baptist Church, Bristol. But that's where this fresh appreciation of an awe-inspiring Gospel started, and I'm so grateful for the patience and encouragement of the church family I've had the privilege of leading for over two decades. They're good listeners and appliers. I've also been deeply blessed, challenged and helped by a variety of staff colleagues, most notably Steve T., Mark L., Richard L., Mark D. and Steve W., and am grateful for all their input into this book and into my life. My hope is that those who read through John's Gospel (either on their own or with others) will find this slim volume of some help in keeping their eyes fixed on John's big picture and so, in turn, on the Saviour himself. Finally, I want to record my immense gratitude, not only to the grace of God that rescued me, but also to the love of Kath that blesses me. A man is blessed indeed to be married to his best friend.

List of Bible abbreviations

THE OLD TESTAMENT		1 Chr.	1 Chronicles	Dan.	Daniel
		2 Chr.	2 Chronicles	Hosea	Hosea
Gen.	Genesis	Ezra	Ezra	Joel	Joel
Exod.	Exodus	Neh.	Nehemiah	Amos	Amos
Lev.	Leviticus	Esth.	Esther	Obad.	Obadiah
Num.	Numbers	Job	Job	Jonah	Jonah
Deut.	Deuteronomy	Ps.	Psalms	Micah	Micah
Josh.	Joshua	Prov.	Proverbs	Nahum	Nahum
Judg.	Judges	Eccles.	Ecclesiastes	Hab.	Habakkuk
Ruth	Ruth	S.of S.	Song of Solomon	Zeph.	Zephaniah
1 Sam.	1 Samuel	Isa.	Isaiah	Hag.	Haggai
2 Sam.	2 Samuel	Jer.	Jeremiah	Zech.	Zechariah
1 Kings	1 Kings	Lam.	Lamentations	Mal.	Malachi
2 Kings	2 Kings	Ezek.	Ezekiel		

THE NEW TESTAMENT		Gal.	Galatians	Heb.	Hebrews
		Eph.	Ephesians	James	James
Matt.	Matthew	Phil.	Philippians	1 Peter	1 Peter
Mark	Mark	Col.	Colossians	2 Peter	2 Peter
Luke	Luke	1 Thes.	1 Thessalonians	1 John	1 John
John	John	2 Thes.	2 Thessalonians	2 John	2 John
Acts	Acts	1 Tim.	1 Timothy	3 John	3 John
Rom.	Romans	2 Tim.	2 Timothy	Jude	Jude
1 Cor.	1 Corinthians	Titus	Titus	Rev.	Revelation
2 Cor.	2 Corinthians	Philem.	Philemon		

Contents

12

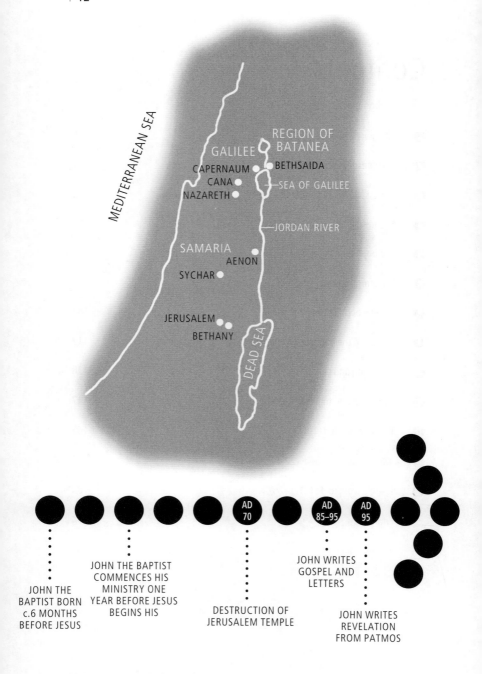

MEDITERRANEAN SEA

REGION OF
BATANEA

GALILEE
CAPERNAUM — BETHSAIDA
CANA
NAZARETH — SEA OF GALILEE

— JORDAN RIVER

SAMARIA
AENON
SYCHAR

JERUSALEM
BETHANY

DEAD SEA

AD 70

AD 85–95

AD 95

JOHN THE
BAPTIST BORN
c.6 MONTHS
BEFORE JESUS

JOHN THE BAPTIST
COMMENCES HIS
MINISTRY ONE
YEAR BEFORE JESUS
BEGINS HIS

DESTRUCTION OF
JERUSALEM TEMPLE

JOHN WRITES
GOSPEL AND
LETTERS

JOHN WRITES
REVELATION
FROM PATMOS

OPENING UP JOHN'S GOSPEL

Background and summary

Towards the end of this Gospel, we are told why it was written. Knowing this shapes and controls everything we read from the beginning: 'But these are written that you may believe that Jesus is the Christ, the Son of God, and that by believing you may have life in his name' (John 20:31).

The author of these words is the apostle John, brother of James, son of Zebedee, and writer of three further Bible letters as well as Revelation. His identity is confirmed by strong early church tradition and by numerous 'internal' characteristics. Significantly, although John is mentioned about twenty times by the other Gospel writers, his name is missing in this Gospel. This fits in well with a writer who emerges as humble and self-effacing.

John's purpose in writing this Gospel is that we may have faith in Jesus. This means that he will provide us with carefully selected evidence (what some call 'signs') to encourage belief. Although he wrote in the context of a multi-cultural, multi-faith Roman Empire, probably around the year AD 85 (and used many symbols and concepts familiar to non-Jews of his day), his concern was to establish truths that primarily impacted a Jewish audience. So we need to be on the lookout for words, stories and references that have a specific Jewish flavour to them.

Red-hot nationalism helped shape first-century Israel. The Maccabean revolt had helped eject the Greeks in 164 BC but the controlling Hasmonean family dynasty (of whom Herod the Great was the last significant member) was increasingly compromised by pagan culture and then by the occupying Roman superpower. How could Israel retain its unique identity? The Pharisees emphasized adherence to religious laws; the Sadducees counselled caution and compromise; the Essenes withdrew into closed communities; and the Zealots (among whom were many Pharisees) advocated violent resistance. And into this heady mix entered the carpenter's son from Nazareth announcing the arrival of the kingdom of God. Little wonder that John's Gospel places such stress on Jesus clarifying what the real nature of this kingdom (and his Messiahship) really were.

Most scholars are agreed that John wrote sometime after the other Gospel writers had completed their accounts, and that not only was he aware of them, but he also assumed his readers were as well. He writes with the authenticity and immediacy of an eyewitness and provides certain details and information that we don't get from Matthew, Mark or Luke. He keeps our focus on Jesus—what he did and what he said—and throughout the Gospel keeps underlining how the power and authority of Christ were clearly evident.

The faith that John wants to encourage in his readers is much more than intellectual assent to certain truths. The evidence that leads to faith must also result in life—'and that by believing you may have life in his name'. This life comes through a new birth (3:3), produces a full experience (10:10), and results in an eternal kingdom (10:28).

1 The glory of God revealed in Jesus

(1:1–51)

Forget your ideas about Jesus the philosopher, or Jesus the example, or Jesus the moralist. If you want to know who Jesus really is, then you have to grasp that he is nothing less than God.

And so, without apology or preparation, John launches his Gospel account straight into truths about God that will stretch and exhaust the deepest thinker. Of all the Gospel writers, John most clearly presents Jesus as the great Creator God of the universe. Understanding who he is and what he has done will lead you to profound wonder and worship.

The Word became flesh (1:1–18)

John uses two symbols, or pictures, to help us understand something about Jesus and about God. He tells us that Jesus is the 'Word' and the 'light'.

Jesus the 'Word': the Word reveals God

A lot has been written about these famous opening verses

but really it all boils down to this—John calls Jesus the 'Word' because it's a special way of saying that Jesus is the one who makes God known. Do you want to know what God is like? asks John. Then take a good look at Jesus.

There are some things about God that can't be immediately understood when we look at the flesh-and-blood Jesus—for example, that God is the eternal Creator, the source of all physical and spiritual life. That is why John puts together his opening sentences as he does, emphasizing these attributes (vv. 1–3).

Jesus the 'light': the light removes darkness

This is a recurring image in John. It helps us answer one obvious question: If Jesus the Word is the one who reveals God, then why doesn't everyone see that? Shouldn't it be obvious?

Why don't people recognize their Creator? Because they live in the darkness. Why didn't all the Jews recognize their promised Messiah? Because they lived in the darkness. Yet Jesus came to remove the darkness and open eyes; he came to show the glory of God and the way of rescue. Do you know why God would act in such a way for rebel people? Have a look at Jesus—he reveals what God is really like. Through him God's grace shines out (v. 14). That's why Jesus came from God to rescue us: God is a God of grace (vv. 12–13).

The Lamb of God (1:19–36)

John supplements the symbols of 'Word' and 'light' with two additional titles: 'the Son of God' and 'the Lamb of God' (vv. 34–36).

A title of position: the 'Son of God'

The title used here must be interpreted in the context of what has already been revealed.

Jesus, being fully divine, became, at the same time, fully human (v. 18). He is as much God as the Father is God; equal but distinct. So when John the apostle quotes John the Baptist saying that Jesus is the Son of God (v. 34), we are obviously meant to understand it in a particular way. This Jesus is no mere man. This Jesus is actually God. When the people saw Jesus, they saw God in human flesh.

This is astounding. John expects us to believe not only that there is but one God, but also that Jesus is as truly God as is the heavenly Father. How can it be humanly reconciled or understood? It has to come to us by revelation from God himself. So as we come to deal with the truth that Jesus Christ is declared to be eternally God and at the same time truly human, we are dealing with a truth that brings to a climax centuries of revelation and leads to wonder, amazement and praise.

A title of purpose: the 'Lamb of God'

John the Baptist calls Jesus the 'Lamb of God' on two occasions (vv. 29, 36). This description must have meant something to his Jewish followers or John would never have used it so pointedly. They might have thought of the lamb that was sacrificed by Abraham so his son could go free (Gen. 22). They might have thought of the Passover lamb—killed so Israel could be set free from slavery (Exod. 12). They might have thought of the lambs sacrificed in the temple morning and evening for the sins of Israel (see, for example, Lev. 14; Num. 6). They might have thought of the lamb described by Isaiah in chapter 53, who was to carry the punishment of sinners. Whichever image came to mind, the lambs had one thing in common—they were sacrificed to deliver people from slavery and set them free from sin.

So when John the Baptist pointed at Jesus and said, 'Look, the Lamb of God, who takes away the sin of the world!', there was no mistaking what he was saying. This Jesus, who was walking towards them, was God's perfect fulfilment of all these pictures, pointers and prophecies about the one who would deliver people from their sin and its consequences. This Jesus was going to be the final, perfect, once-for-all sacrifice for sin.

The calling of the first disciples (1:37–51)

You can sense John's passion to make Jesus known, and you can detect his delight at recounting how he and Andrew came to meet Jesus in the first place (there is no 'proof' that this passage describes John's first meeting of Jesus, but he is the one traditionally identified. Specific references (such as the time given in 1:39) seem to indicate that this is an eyewitness account). One phrase is repeated in this passage: Jesus said to Andrew and John, 'Come and see.' Philip said to Nathanael, 'Come and see.' And such has been the potently effective tool of Christian mission, the invitation to 'come and see'.

> Such has been the potently effective tool of Christian mission, the invitation to 'come and see'.

John includes for us the account of how Philip was instrumental in introducing Jesus to Nathanael (vv. 44–51). Nathanael started as one of the most sceptical people about Jesus before becoming one of his most convinced followers, calling Jesus 'the Son of God ... the King of Israel' (v. 49). You can't get titles any higher than that. To Nathanael, Jesus is nothing less than the Messiah-Deliverer who is to come and eject the occupying Roman forces and restore a golden age of Jewish self-government. That is the best anyone could ever do, Nathanael thinks. He can't think outside that idea of political deliverance.

Notice how Jesus answers him (vv. 50–51). It's as if Jesus is saying to him, 'Nathanael, what I am going to do will astound you. It's going to be bigger than anything you can ever imagine.' And to reinforce his point, Jesus makes a reference that Jewish readers will immediately have understood. In verse 51, he refers to an incident in the life of Jacob, when he ran away and had a dream of a ladder to heaven (see Gen. 28:12).

Jesus is claiming that he not only reveals God (that is, brings God to us), but he also opens the way up into God's presence (that is, brings us to God). He is the ladder. He (in the words of Jacob) is the stairway to heaven. And that, says Jesus to Nathanael, is something bigger than you could ever imagine, bigger even than the national deliverance of Israel.

For further study ▶

1. Where does the description of the 'lamb of God' appear in the Old Testament? How is it used?
2. Look at John 1:17. Is John contrasting 'law' and 'grace'?
3. Read about Jacob's ladder in Genesis 28:12. How does Jesus fit into this imagery?

TO THINK ABOUT AND DISCUSS

1. Look again at John 1:1–18. Why didn't John just write that 'Jesus is God'?
2. Think about how Andrew told his brother about Jesus (vv. 40–42). Although John didn't intend Andrew to be the definitive model for personal evangelism, are there things that we can learn from him?
3. What was Nathanael's mistake in verse 46? Can we ever be guilty of this?

2 The unexpected Messiah

(2:1–3:36)

'You're not what I was expecting' is frequently heard on doorsteps. The person standing before them doesn't seem to match the voice that had been heard on the phone or the impression gained from the email. And Jesus certainly doesn't fit the identikit picture that has been drawn up over centuries of Jewish history of the 'Messiah' they were expecting. So the lesson begins in an obscure village in Galilee.

Water into wine (2:1–11)

Jesus, along with six of his disciples, has been invited to a wedding. Mary his mother may well have been helping with the catering and she sees that the wine has run out. She knows that this reflects very badly on the groom and will bring disgrace on his family. So she involves Jesus, who gently rebukes her for drawing him in. As a result, Jesus orders that six huge stone jars should be topped up with water. He then orders that some should be drawn out and given to the Master of Ceremonies, who discovers that, not only has Jesus changed that water into wine, but it's top-quality stuff, and there's over 500 litres of it!

At first reading, it seems that John wants us to understand that Jesus can do some remarkable miracles. But John doesn't use the Greek word that means 'powerful miracle'; he uses a word that means 'sign' (v. 11). So there's more to this than first meets the eye. John is telling us that this miracle is a signpost to more than just the power of God. As he continues in verse 11: 'He thus revealed his glory, and his disciples put their faith in him.'

It's about wine

Wine was a symbol to the Jewish people of times of plenty and blessing. Their own scriptures were full of prophecies and promises about the time when there would be lots of wine.

So the Jewish readers in particular would have seen that Jesus was fulfilling Old Testament prophecies. God's kingdom was breaking through. This was a pointer to the joy and gladness and super-abundance that characterizes God's goodness to his people. We also need to see what the wine replaced, because John points out where this wine came from (v. 6). Look at Mark 7:3–4.

These were jars from which servants would draw water, which in turn was then poured over the hands of those who came to eat. This wasn't simply about washing their hands before dinner; this was a religious ceremony. And what does Jesus do? He replaces the ceremonial water with wine. Symbolically, he replaces the old religion of religious rituals with the new wine of a joyful relationship.

When Jesus reigns in a life, the best image to describe it is not the mourning of a funeral but the celebration of a party. Little wonder some of the older Christian songs have lines like 'Religion never was designed to make our pleasures less' (Isaac Watts, from 'Come, We that Love the Lord') and 'Solid joys and lasting treasure, none but Zion's children know' (John Newton, from 'Glorious Things of Thee are Spoken').

It's about when

If you were reading John's Gospel for the first time and didn't know how it ended, you might have been confused by what Jesus said when speaking to his mother (v. 4). What does 'My time has not yet come' mean? In one sense we know the answer, because we know what the climax of the Gospel is: the death and resurrection of Jesus. In John 12:23 we see how this expression refers to Christ's death.

Jesus was pointing out that what he came to do could be put into the category of 'Now, but not yet'. The miracle of the abundant wine was fulfilling prophecies made to describe the wonders of God's kingdom, but it was only a partial fulfilment. The new wine eventually ran out. But that real, actual, substantial kingdom where Jesus will perfectly reign was still to come. So what we have here is the 'Now, but not yet'.

Temple business (2:12–25)

The temple in Jerusalem was incredibly important to the

Jewish people; it was the place that symbolized where they could go and meet God. It was also the place where all the sacrifices were made. But what had happened was that the religious rulers had made a business out of people meeting with God. They would sell to them (at a good profit, of course) animals that they could sacrifice. In one sense this was quite reasonable, as people would travel considerable distances to be there and this saved them the bother of bringing with them one of their own animals. But if you wanted to buy one of these animals (and, in fact, only these animals were allowed for sacrifice), you needed to change your money into the only currency authorized by the Jewish rules. So they also provided money changers, who in turn happened to charge a huge rate of commission. And the place where they carried out this exploitative business was the area of the temple known as the Court of the Gentiles. This was supposed to be where seeking Gentiles could come and find out about God, but now it was a religious supermarket. Instead of being a place of prayer and seeking, it had become a cattle market filled with cash registers.

So Jesus responded by driving out these profiteers (vv. 14–16). What's amazing is that the Jewish authorities didn't complain about what Jesus did. Instead, some of the Jews realized that this was actually what God had promised would happen when the Messiah came (see Mal. 3:1–4). And some of the disciples remembered that this was what was promised about the Messiah in Psalm 69:9; 'His disciples remembered that it is written, "Zeal for your house will consume me"' (John 2:17).

Notice not only *where* this all took place, but also *when* it took place. John tells us it was the time of the Jewish Passover (v. 13). This was the time when Jewish people remembered being set free from slavery in Egypt. And in Christ's day there was heightened expectation that something would happen to the occupying Roman army and that Israel would be delivered.

So the questions began to fly. Was this Jesus the Messiah? Was he going to be the one to throw out the Romans? And the answer that came back was 'no'—he was going to be the one who threw out fake religion instead. It wasn't Romans he threw out but those who got in the way of people coming close to God. The slavery of sin is far worse than political oppression. And this becomes clearer as we see how John records some wordplay from Jesus that deliberately confused some but became transparently clear for others (vv. 18–21).

> The slavery of sin is far worse than political oppression.

Some words that Jesus used here could be used in connection with either a physical body or a brick building. Jesus was comparing his body to the amazing temple in Jerusalem. Remember that the temple was the place to which people could go to meet God. So Jesus was strongly hinting that he was the one through whom people could come to meet God.

That's why he said, 'Destroy this temple, and I will raise it again in three days.' This, of course, was precisely what happened. Jesus was crucified on a cross three years later outside the city walls of Jerusalem and rose from the dead on the third day. And later, as they looked back, the disciples saw the full significance of these words.

Jesus teaches Nicodemus (3:1–13)

Nicodemus was from one of the strictest religious groups in the whole of Israel. Jesus describes him as '*the* teacher of Israel' (literal translation of v. 10). He was considered to be one of the wisest religious men in Judaism. He knew his Bible better than anyone. But he didn't get it. What was confusing Nicodemus was this teacher called Jesus. Some people had started to wonder whether he was the promised Messiah—the one who would lead Israel into a new age of power and wealth. And now Nicodemus had the opportunity to observe this Jesus first-hand. Although Jesus had been operating out of the northern region called Galilee, he had come south for the Passover and was staying in Jerusalem. And what Nicodemus witnessed there suggested to him that this Jesus might indeed be the real article.

You can see where his questions are going. 'Rabbi, there's something very special about you. You must be from God because of the signs and miracles that we have witnessed. But if you are the Messiah, where's this kingdom that God promised? I don't get it.'

But as Jesus makes clear, the problem is of his own making. Although he is the top teacher of the Scriptures in his country, Nicodemus hasn't understood what those Scriptures have been saying. So in his answer, Jesus refers back to amazing promises made in Ezekiel (36:25–27; 37:9–10) about the new kingdom that God would bring about for his people.

This is why Nicodemus doesn't get it. Nicodemus is only

able to think of God's kingdom in terms of political parties that will rule, wealth you can count, and religion that is performed, whereas Jesus is saying to Nicodemus, 'Don't you get it? God's kingdom is a spiritual kingdom. It's not to do with outward performance, it's to do with an inward change. The place where God must rule is not primarily from palaces and parliaments, it's primarily in the heart and soul, because the problem is not occupying armies, it's occupying sin. So, Nicodemus, if you want to be part of God's kingdom, if you want your sin removed, you must be born again. God himself must change you from the inside. God himself must give you a new beginning. So what, Nicodemus, if you know your Bible backwards—that's not going to bring about the change on the inside that is essential—you must be born again.'

> The place where God must rule is not primarily from palaces and parliaments, it's primarily in the heart and soul, because the problem is not occupying armies, it's occupying sin.

Key words (3:14–16)

But that creates problems for Nicodemus; he can think only in terms of performing religious duties and conforming to religious codes. He can't take in the idea that a new start is essential. So in verse 9 he asks, 'How can this be?' Jesus answers by using an incident from Israel's history that is familiar to Nicodemus. And then, in verse 16, John adds his own interpretive comments;[1] words that have become probably the most famous and most repeated of the entire Bible.

Although God had done astounding things for the exodus Israelites, they moaned about their conditions. And as a judgement on their rebellion, God sent poisonous snakes into their camp, which bit the people and led to death (see Num. 21:4–9). That's why, when John goes on to write 'For God so loved the world' in John 3:16, he doesn't use a word that means 'planet', including all the wonders of nature and creation, he uses a word that was generally employed to indicate wickedness and failure.

What is being pointed to is the fact that we've all got a problem that can't be solved by our own efforts. We live in disobedience to God. It's like a deadly poison coursing through our veins. The only hope is for a radical solution that will bring about a complete change.

God told Moses to construct a bronze snake, put it on a pole and lift it up; and those who looked to it for life would live. And, of course, that's exactly what Jesus said was going to happen to him. He was going to be pinned to a cross and lifted up on Calvary so that all who looked to him in faith would live.

Light and love (3:17–21)

The world is divided into two camps—those who through faith in Jesus have been rescued and have entered into God's mercy and love, and those upon whom God's holy and just condemnation is burning down at this very moment.

Now this is so plainly shocking and disturbing that many today will not say anything about it.

The biggest issue facing all living souls is where they stand before God. Have they put their faith in God's appointed rescuer, his own Son Jesus Christ, or does his just and holy condemnation rest upon them at this very moment? This is so vital an issue that John goes on to give two tests as to whether a person lives under grace or under condemnation.

The first test, in verse 20, tells us that those who are under God's condemnation don't want to expose their lives to the light of God's character or God's Word. They're afraid of what it will show up. They know the comparison will be to their detriment.

The second test is in verse 21. John is not saying that someone who has been rescued by God becomes a do-gooding show-off. Rather he says that the rescued person wants to make sure that everyone can see that God has done it. That person wants the glory and the honour to go to God, not to him- or herself.

John the Baptizer's humble testimony (3:22–36)

Jesus has been in Jerusalem for the Passover celebrations, he has been visited by the leading Jewish teacher, and now he and his followers travel out of Jerusalem, moving north-east towards the Jordan River. They settle for some time near to where John the Baptist is working. And while they are there, the followers of John the Baptist have occasion to draw their master's attention to the contrasting popularity between himself and Jesus (v. 26). John's reaction and response to this reveals what should be true of any Christian worker.

In verses 27–28, John the Baptist is saying that God's servants can only do that which God has called them to do. It isn't down to him which path in life he should pursue; rather, what matters most is his obedience to the call of God.

It's never easy to be told that others are doing better than you. It requires a mountain of humility to rejoice with others who are prospering when you are stagnating. In one sense, this was John's experience. At one time, large crowds had flocked to hear him and he was the talk of Jerusalem; once, people even wondered if he was the promised Messiah. But now those crowds were thinning out and going over to hear Jesus and spend time in his company. How did he cope with it? What was his response? In verses 29b–30, it's a response of joy. Here is the mark of a godly person: 'He must become greater; I must become less.'

> It requires a mountain of humility to rejoice with others who are prospering when you are stagnating.

Listen to the words of James Denney: 'You cannot at the same time give the impression that you are a great preacher and that Jesus Christ is a great Savior.'[2] And the observation of Jim Packer: 'If you call attention to yourself and your own competence, you cannot effectively call attention to Jesus and his glorious sufficiency.'[3]

To help his followers understand how he viewed his ministry, John the Baptist used two images. Firstly, he used the image of a wedding. Jesus was the bridegroom, he said, and John was like the best man, preparing the way for his friend. So John's real delight was that, after he had made the arrangements, the bridegroom had arrived, the wedding could commence, the union could be effected and the joy could be experienced. As best man he moved out of the picture, delighted to keep the happy couple in focus. Look at them, he said, not me.

But the second image John alluded to is not as immediately obvious. It's the contrast between an eyewitness and a barrister. In a law court, the greatest authority lies with the eyewitnesses. They know what they have seen. Their testimonies are, therefore, immensely powerful and credible. The barrister, on the other hand, hasn't seen these things for himself. Instead he represents and speaks on behalf of another. This is what John suggests in verses 31–33. That's another reason, John says, why Jesus is greater. He is the absolutely truthful and reliable eyewitness. In contrast, John describes himself as the one who 'speaks as one from the earth'.

The words written at the end of the chapter are either a summary of what John the Baptist said, or are the apostle John's observations; we don't know for sure. But what is abundantly clear is the passion that all those who hear these words will respond to them (v. 36). They repeat the theme that has been running through the chapter.

For further study ▶

FOR FURTHER STUDY

1. Study the imagery of wine in Amos 9:13–15; Jeremiah 31:11–14; Isaiah 25:6–9; Joel 2:19, 23–24. What does it represent?
2. Have a look at Malachi 3:1–4. How did Jesus fulfil this prophecy when he visited the temple?
3. Read Ezekiel 36:25–27 and 37:9–10. What should Nicodemus have understood from these passages?

TO THINK ABOUT AND DISCUSS

1. Why is joy so rarely associated with the Christian life today? Are there obstacles in the way of our experiencing or demonstrating it?
2. How many times does the word 'believe' occur in John 3:1–36? Why does it occur so frequently?
3. Have you ever been tempted to criticize other people (or churches) that seem to be prospering more than you? Can you rejoice in the blessings of others? Are there things you need to learn from John the Baptist's attitude to Jesus?

3 A message for all people

(4:1–5:47)

In John 3, we saw how Jesus met with a Jewish leader called Nicodemus—a good, religious man, the sort of man you think would suit church: a decent, moral, 'knows his Bible' type of man. But what Jesus emphasized was that the new life that God provides is not dependent upon your background, upbringing or behaviour, but is a gift from God given to 'whoever' will believe. The next person that Jesus encountered was in direct contrast with Nicodemus.

A Samaritan woman (4:1–26)

Whereas Nicodemus was a man, it is now a woman Jesus meets and talks to. In Western society today, we fail to see the immense significance of this fact. We live in an age of relative equality and respect. But Jesus worked in a culture in which women were looked down upon. They had no property rights, they couldn't give evidence in a law court, and some Jews thought that it was a waste of time for a rabbi to talk with a woman, even his own wife, because it would divert him from studying the Torah, the Jewish rule book. Others believed that giving your daughters a knowledge of that book was as inappropriate as selling them into prostitution. And all the men daily thanked God in their prayers that they hadn't been made female.

We also notice that Nicodemus was Jewish, whereas the woman was a Samaritan. Once again, we have to work hard to understand something of the intense racial hatred that there was between these two groups. The travelling details given in verses 3–4 are there because John's Jewish readers would never have gone through Samaria to get to Galilee, even though it was the most direct route. That's why the Samaritan woman is surprised that Jesus talks to her (v. 9).

Notice the final contrast that John draws our attention to. Nicodemus was a highly religious and respected leader, but this woman was a moral outcast (vv. 16–18). That's the very reason why she came to draw water from that well at midday. No woman in her right mind would ordinarily do that—the heat would have been stifling. The women from the town would have come early morning or in the cool of the evening—but this woman wanted to avoid them and their stares and gossip, so she came at midday. You can imagine the sort of talk that went flying around the town. 'She's the whore, the scarlet woman, the woman who can't keep her man. Watch out, girls—she'll be after your husbands next.' Vicious, ugly, painful gossip. But Jesus spoke to her and offered her that new, born-again life that would thoroughly satisfy.

So John is making it very clear to his readers that when Jesus said that 'whoever' can have eternal life, he meant 'whoever'—even that adulterous Samaritan woman became a believer in Jesus Christ. She experienced a new start, cleansing from guilt and acceptance from God.

But as well as drawing this contrast, John is also illustrating the satisfaction that Jesus brings to empty, disappointed people. It was precisely that feeling that Jesus addressed when he talked to this Samaritan. She'd gone there at noon to draw water and met Jesus taking a rest from his journey, feeling tired and thirsty. So naturally their conversation turned to the theme of water, and Jesus made a remarkable statement (vv. 13–14).

At first, the woman didn't understand what he was getting at. She thought he was still talking about some strange water that you could drink, but as the story continues it becomes obvious that Jesus was using the picture of water to represent that eternally satisfying life that only God can provide.

There are a couple of things that we don't immediately grasp as we read this story 2,000 years later in our comfortable, high-tech, pagan culture. The first is how absolutely vital water was to that Middle Eastern society. If you couldn't get access to water your crops would fail, your flocks would die of thirst, and you and your family would perish. That's why water supplies were so crucial. Of course, the opposite was also true. If you had a plentiful supply of water, you would prosper. Your crops would grow, your flocks would multiply, and your wealth and health would increase. So to have a supply of water that would never fail was the Middle Eastern idea of the greatest blessing you could experience. And this idea of deep satisfaction and joy was partly what Jesus was getting at here.

But secondly, as with much of John's Gospel, there are images here that would have been familiar to the Jewish reader that are not so familiar to us today. Look at Jeremiah 2:13 and Isaiah 55:1–2.

> The trouble was, this woman was looking for that satisfaction in her own way, not God's way.

Jesus was telling the woman that he was able to give her the joy, peace, satisfaction and meaning to her life that she so desperately craved. The trouble was, this woman was looking for that satisfaction in her own way, not God's way. Like the rest of humanity, she had rejected the spring of living water (that is, God) and had dug her own well, which was totally unable to hold the water she was thirsty for.

But in response to Jesus exposing the fact that she was looking for satisfaction in all the wrong places, she started to argue religion with him. She wanted to discuss the relative merits of whether you should worship God on Mount Gerizim (as the Samaritans said) or in Jerusalem (as the Jews had argued). But even though this had been an important question up till now, Jesus would have none of it. The issue was not whether God was limited to one place or another; the real issue was what God was really like (v. 22).

Jesus implied that it wasn't good enough for the

Samaritans to make up their own ideas about God; they had to find out what God had actually revealed about himself. He pointed to one particular attribute (v. 24) to show that God can't be confined to a place in the way you can confine a statue or an idol to one place at one time. Nor can God be controlled or manipulated any more than you can go outside and change the direction the wind is blowing. He is spirit. He is quite other from us. He does not share our limitations or frailties. Indeed, when the word 'Spirit' is used of God in the Old Testament, it describes his amazing, creative, life-giving power.

But Jesus didn't stop there. There was more that the woman had to know if she was to understand who God is. Because, in one sense, how can you know and have a relationship with a God who is spirit? How can our separating sins ever be dealt with?

Jesus gave a couple of heavily loaded clues in verses 21 and 23. He said that something was going to happen very soon that would make it possible for people to worship and enjoy God in the way that he intended; not in a way that was limited to particular mountains or towns, but something that could touch all individuals, whoever they were and wherever they lived.

And what was this thing? Whenever we find the expression about the 'time coming' in John's Gospel, it's all to do with the crucifixion of Jesus (8:20; 12:23–24; 13:1; 17:1). Jesus was saying that, if people truly want to worship and enjoy the living and true God, then there is one way that they can come, and that is through him and the way that he would open up on the cross.

So what was it that Jesus told the Samaritan woman by way of response? That the only way to worship God is in truth. You can't make up God. You must listen to God's own self-revelation, both through the Bible and through his Son, Jesus Christ. And the only way to worship God is in spirit, not through outward, formal, meaningless rituals and ceremonies, but in a way that engages the very deepest level of your being.

The disciples return to learn a lesson (4:27–42)

The disciples return to the well to discover (to their great surprise) Jesus talking with a Samaritan woman. They have not seen how Jesus has dealt with her nor heard the answers he has given. So it is their turn to learn some vital lessons.

We have already noted the immense religious and cultural divide that existed between the Jews and the Samaritans. There were lessons to learn in this, and through the example of Jesus the disciples were confronted with the issue of their own prejudice.

No doubt Jesus was both hungry and thirsty. That was the reason why the disciples had gone into Sychar—so that they could bring back food for their master. But the response of Jesus pointed them towards the necessity of concentrating on what really matters. For Jesus, what was most important to him, even above taking in life-sustaining food, was to do what God had called him to do. That was his goal and vision; it was literally his life-consuming passion.

This was a lesson that the disciples had to learn. They'd started following Jesus with an eye to the rewards that following the Jewish Messiah would bring. They dreamt of power and financial reward. They imagined the prestige that would follow their obedience. But their tired and hungry master, ministering to an adulterous Samaritan woman and about to be swamped by the approaching villagers, reminded them what was most important. Jesus said that nothing is more important than doing what God wants you to do (vv. 34–35).

> Jesus said that nothing is more important than doing what God wants you to do.

Once again, Jesus alluded to verses in the Old Testament as he saw the people from Sychar streaming out to meet him. He used harvest language that would have had special significance to his disciples because of their Jewish upbringing. 'Look at the fields,' he said, 'they are ripe for harvest.' This harvesting imagery was associated with the coming kingdom of God (see Amos 9:13).

This coming kingdom, in which people would be gathered from all corners of the globe, was now beginning to break through. Even Samaritans were being saved and rescued. And the invitation of Jesus to his disciples was to get involved in the climax of God's purposes for the world. 'This is it,' said Jesus, 'this is what was promised long ago. This is what God has been preparing down through the ages. The sowing of biblical revelation has now reached its climax.' As he said in verse 38, 'I sent you to reap what you have not worked for. Others have done the hard work, and you have reaped the benefits of their labour.'

To get involved in serving King Jesus is nothing less than being part of the greatest plan the universe has ever seen: the rescue and glorification of God's children. But this image of a ripe harvest in the Old Testament not only referred to God's people being gathered into his kingdom, but also to God's judgement upon those who reject him (see Joel 3:13–14).

Faith and healing (4:43–54)

When Jesus returns to the area in which he has settled, northern Galilee, he is faced with a different response from that in Samaria. The Galilean Jews have witnessed amazing miracles—back at the beginning of John 2 we noticed how Jesus changed water into wine at a wedding. And many of them were present in Jerusalem for the Passover feast and have seen Jesus perform other miraculous signs. But it seems that all they are interested in is the entertainment value they can get out of Jesus. They want another miracle; they want to be amazed and have a free drink or a free meal, but they don't take notice of what the miracles mean or to what they are pointing.

This seems to explain the sarcasm that John uses in verses 44–45: 'the Galileans welcomed him'—yes, but for all the wrong reasons. So that when we come to verse 48, we find Jesus making this complaint to the people about the way that they view him: 'Unless you people see miraculous signs and wonders, you will never believe.'

This was the problem. The evidence was there. Jesus had been fulfilling the promises made about the Messiah in the Jewish scriptures. He had been performing miracles that pointed to his unique and divine authority. But they just didn't see it. They didn't look at where the signs were pointing; they just looked out for their own self-interest.

But there was one man who was different. He hadn't come to be entertained or titillated. This man was in desperate need. His son was dying. And although he was a high-ranking official in the government, well able to afford the best doctors and latest treatments, nothing was working. His only hope lay in this Jesus. If his son was to live, only one man could bring about the miraculous cure. And so he came—not to gape in wonder but to plead in desperation. He wanted a miracle—not for its entertainment value but for its healing power.

He asked Jesus to accompany him back to his house in Capernaum and do something miraculous in front of them that would cure his boy. So what did Jesus do? In his great compassion, he did something about it, but not by way of a miracle that others could applaud and be entertained by. Rather he just assured the man of his son's healing: 'You may go. Your son will live.' That's it. Nothing showy. Just his words. And the man's response? 'The man took Jesus at his word and departed.'

How significant this is! Jesus has complained to the people that they are obsessed by the miracles without being able to see what they are pointing to. But here we have a man who has seen. He's looked at the signs and seen where they've been pointing. He's seen that they reveal that Jesus is none other than the Son of God, the promised Messiah. And as a result he trusts what Jesus says. It doesn't matter to him that there is no outward spectacular miracle—it is enough that Jesus has told him that his son will live! If Jesus has said it, then what he has said can be trusted absolutely.

And, of course, we know how the story ends (vv. 51–53).

It wasn't just the man who believed; it was now everyone in his home. They heard his story and acknowledged the power and authority of King Jesus.

Healing at the pool (5:1–15)

Who are we to listen to? Where does truth lie? Should we go on living the way we are, or should we change the way we think and live? This is the essence of the argument that fills John 5. The first four chapters have introduced Jesus. We've seen his miracles, noted his character, and listened to his teaching. But now the opposition kicks in. And John shows us that, as a result of three major healing miracles Jesus performed—healing an invalid in chapter 5, giving sight to a blind man in chapter 9, and raising a dead man to life in chapter 11—major opposition was revealed from the Jewish authorities.

The big question they posed to Jesus was this: Why should we do what you say? What authority do you have? Why should we change?

In John 5:1–15, John paints a graphic scene for us. There's the pool, surrounded by five great colonnades. In the background there's the bleating of sheep as they are led through the Sheep Gate into the temple compound for sacrifice. And filling the view is a crowd of disabled people—not neatly dressed or sitting in wheelchairs, but, for the most part, outcasts and beggars, sprawling over the area wearing rags. Some can't see, some can't walk, some can't move. The smell is overpowering. The sight is pitiful in the extreme. And they're waiting for something to happen. They've been told that when the water stirs of its own accord—as it will, being a seasonal spring fed from the hills around Jerusalem—then the first one in will be healed.

And of all the sick and disabled who crowd into this area, Jesus finds one of the most pitiful—someone who has been coming here for thirty-eight years, a paralysed man who has no help or support. And Jesus speaks just a few words to him: 'Get up! Pick up your mat and walk' (v. 8). And what happens? 'At once the man was cured; he picked up his mat and walked' (v. 9).

'At once'! John doesn't usually emphasize this aspect of Jesus's miracles, but he does here. Do you realize how remarkable this miracle was? If someone today had corrective surgery to enable him or her to walk after thirty-eight years of paralysis, that person would have to undergo a course of physiotherapy to restore muscle tone. But what happened here? It was so thorough—so complete. Not only was the paralysis dealt with, but the strength was immediately restored: 'he picked up his mat and walked.'

So John is deliberately emphasizing for us the supernatural nature of this healing. And if we follow the story through, we will see why. In verse 10, we read that the Jews said, 'It is the Sabbath; the law forbids you to carry your mat.' Now, this is the heart of the matter. In fact, the law they were referring to was not from the Old Testament, as this man did not normally carry mats around for a living; this law came from their own rule book, in which rabbis had determined that there were thirty-nine different categories of work that were not allowed on their special Sabbath day. This man-made law book was the authority by which the Jewish leaders tried to shape their own lives and the lives of others.

But do you notice the telling reply of the man who had been healed and the authority he quoted (v. 11)? He reasoned that, if this man was able to perform such a supernatural and astounding miracle, he must have had an authority that was more than human. He needed to be listened to. Just look at his credentials. His miracle confirmed his divine nature; therefore, the man reasoned, I'd better do what he said.

John concludes this episode with a fascinating ending (vv. 12–15). Jesus said to the man who had been healed, 'See, you are well again. Stop sinning or something worse may happen to you.' What on earth did Jesus mean, and why did John bother to record this strange exchange in the temple?

The 'something worse' that Jesus was referring to could not be a recurrence of his paralysing disease. In fact, it's difficult to imagine what could ever be physically worse for the man than what he'd already experienced for thirty-eight years. No—the 'something worse' was to do with the soul. Jesus was here referring to being eternally condemned and shut out of the presence of God. That's something far, far worse.

So really Jesus was saying to this man, 'Look, you've had your body made well, but what really matters is the state of your soul. So get right before God—have your sins dealt with; that's far more important than twenty or so more years of reasonable health.'

> Get right before God—have your sins dealt with; that's far more important than twenty or so more years of reasonable health.

The weight of evidence (5:16–47)

Jesus upset a number of religious officials because he told the paralysed man to do something that was forbidden by the Jewish religious code—namely, carry his mat on the Sabbath day, their special day of rest. But in verse 17, this was compounded by his claim to be equal with God, through stating that the Sabbath regulations had no more authority over him than they did over God himself. 'God doesn't stop working on the Sabbath,' said Jesus, 'and so neither do I.' He didn't argue with the Jews over the way they'd misinterpreted what was actually written in the Old Testament; he simply went straight to the heart of things: 'just as God is always working out his purposes, so am I.'

The Jews didn't miss the point; they saw what Jesus was claiming. This was nothing less than a claim to be regarded as equal with God. What the Bible teaches and what Jesus revealed in this passage is an amazing truth that must be received by faith. It defies simple explanations but rewards careful thought. What Jesus explained in his response to the Jews (and what we understand today under the term 'Trinity') is that there are separate persons in the Godhead who at one and the same time are totally interrelated and interdependent. There are not three gods—there is one God; but that one God comprises three distinct but equal and interdependent persons. Notice in verses 19–20 how this was emphasized by Jesus, who corrected the wrong assumptions of the Jews.

While claiming equality with God, Jesus also made clear that what he did was in total obedience to the will of God the Father (v. 19). Everything that Jesus did was in total, complete, absolute conformity with what God the Father decreed. So while Jesus, God the Son, did all that his heavenly Father decreed, God the Father shared with his Son his perfect, infinite love (v. 20).

There were two things, according to the rabbis of the time, that marked out God from humans: firstly, that he alone was the life-giver, and, secondly, that he was the judge of all. These things, the rabbis said, could not be done by any human; they were entirely God's prerogative. (See Deut. 32:39; 2 Kings 5:7; Gen. 18:25.)

So giving life and judging both mark out God from humankind. Now look at what Jesus said in verses 21–22. Jesus was saying that what marked God out as divine also marked *him* out as divine. He then went on to give three proofs of his claim to equality with God, perhaps because the Jewish law in Deuteronomy 19:15 said this: 'One witness is not enough ... A matter must be established by the testimony of two or three witnesses.'

Listen to John's witness

In verses 33–35 Jesus mentioned the official Jewish delegation that was sent from Jerusalem to John the Baptist. We read about it in back in 1:19–20. There, John was explicit in identifying Jesus as the Son of God.

Look at Jesus's works

The second proof concerns the miraculous works Jesus was doing (v. 36). How else can you explain what was happening? It must have been God at work. In fact, the whole context of this discussion was the healing of the paralysed man which no one could dispute; the man was walking around in Jerusalem as they spoke.

Learn from God's words

Jesus said that the Old Testament was continually pointing to him (vv. 37–40). The prophecies about a coming Messiah Saviour were about him. The symbols and ceremonies of the temple—with their sacrifices and high priests—were about him. The historical passages about a rescuer from the enemy were about him. Wherever you might dip into the Old Testament, you would find something about him.

So Jesus set out the evidence. Overwhelming, you might think, but the reality was that the Jewish leaders would not listen. They rejected out of hand what Jesus was saying. And so Jesus went on to outline three major reasons why this was so.

Performance religion

One of the most famous rabbis of that time, Rabbi Hillel, had taught the Jews that by studying the words of the law they would gain for themselves life in the world to come.

He was repeating the age-old theory that still exists today: that if you are religious, you can earn yourself a place in heaven. Little wonder, then, that the teaching of Jesus was an affront to them (v. 39); he taught that salvation came through repentance and faith alone.

Personal interest

Jesus said that people would follow those whose ideas and

teachings best suited their own interests (vv. 43–44), but they would not follow Jesus because his insistence on their inability to save themselves affronted their pride.

Perverse thinking

To the Jews, Moses was the great hero. He was the one who brought them out of Egypt and into their promised land. He was the one who gave them God's law. And the Jewish teachers believed that it was through following Moses that they would be delivered. But Jesus confronted them with the perversity of their thinking (vv. 45–47). Moses gave the law so that the people would realize their failure and inability, seek God's salvation and look for God's deliverer. But what happened? The law became an end in itself, and the Jews rejected the one Moses spoke of and pointed to.

FOR FURTHER STUDY

1. Have a look at Jeremiah 2:13 and Isaiah 55:1–2. How is the imagery of water closely connected to blessing? How else is this water pictured in Ezekiel 43 and 47, and Isaiah 44 and 55?

2. Amos 9:13 gives an example of harvest imagery associated with the coming kingdom of God. Where else in the Old Testament does such imagery occur?

3. Look at Joel 3:12–14. How is harvest also a picture of God's judgement?

4. Read Deuteronomy 32:39; 2 Kings 5:7; Genesis 18:25. Which characteristics of God did Jesus display?

TO THINK ABOUT AND DISCUSS

1. How would you define 'worship'? Is there a danger that our understanding of this word can be shaped more by our upbringing and culture than by Scripture? How?

2. In what ways are you involved in the harvest that Jesus spoke about? Are there groups of people you have considered to be 'beyond the pale'?

3. Why can't many people see that Jesus is equal with God the Father? What would be the implications to them of such belief?

4 The Jewish Saviour

(6:1–8:59)

We're entering a new section for John. He has moved the scene from Jerusalem to Galilee and jumped a period of time (v. 1: 'Some time after this …'). The popularity of Jesus was reaching its peak and a great crowd was following.

Feeding 5,000 (6:1–15)

Passover isn't far off—that special meal always reminded the people of deliverance from an enslaving enemy. Many similarities suggest to the gathering crowds that the occupying Roman army might soon receive the same treatment that Moses dealt out to the Egyptians (see Deut. 18:15; Isa. 11).

They are in a wilderness place (just as with the exodus), they've been divided into numbered groups (just as the exodus), and this great teacher has miraculously provided bread for them to eat (just as God provided manna during the exodus). And what's more, after they collect up the leftovers (as was the Jewish custom), they discover that they have filled *twelve* baskets with bread. A basket for each of the twelve tribes of Israel; everyone sees the significance of that. Surely this is it—the time when Israel will beat the world champions and regain its political and religious independence.

But how does this all end? With a mass uprising making its way to Jerusalem to overthrow the Roman authorities? Read verse 15.

So what was the problem? Why didn't Jesus go along with the crowd? And why did Jesus feed all those people in the first place? And what is it that the writer of this account, the disciple John, wants future readers like us to understand? He identifies three major problems.

Their views of Jesus were too small

Chapter 5 dealt with some very important teachings about who Jesus really was. He claimed equality with God the Father and pointed to evidence to back up those amazing and audacious claims. And now we come to the revision lesson. Jesus wanted to see whether his disciples had really grasped what he was saying: that he was none other than God in human flesh (6:5–6).

We are specifically told that in the crowd there were 5,000 men (that is, males of a fighting age). Commentators assess that the whole crowd therefore probably numbered around 20,000. That was the scene that greeted the disciples and the challenge that Jesus laid before Philip.

And obviously, the human answer was that it was impossible. It could not be done (v. 7)! But what Philip had failed to take into account was that the one before him was

God. Philip thought things through on a purely human level, omitting to take into consideration the infinite power of a gracious God. His view of Jesus was too small, too limiting.

Their desires for themselves were too weak

The attraction of Jesus was not only that he entertained them by astounding miracles, but also that he was someone who helped meet their needs. You didn't need to visit the doctor when Jesus was around; come to that, you didn't need to use the supermarket, either: Jesus would provide you with food for free (vv. 2, 26).

That was the problem. They were preoccupied with the here and now; with their immediate physical needs; with their material problems. But there was so much more that Jesus had come to do for them.

Their hopes for rescue were too limited

The problem was that the Jews assumed that, when their scriptures spoke about a Messiah/Rescuer, they were referring to one who would rescue the nation from its troubles and oppression. They could only view the work of their coming King in terms of victory over political enemies and occupying forces (vv. 14–15). But the lesson that Jesus was teaching and the work he had come to do were so much bigger than that.

The bigger enemy he had

> The greater salvation was not to do with a kingdom that would pass away in time, but with a heavenly kingdom that would last for ever.

come to fight was sin. The bigger problem was mankind's alienation from God. The greater salvation was not to do with a kingdom that would pass away in time, but with a heavenly kingdom that would last for ever. And the greater sphere of his work was to do with all of lost mankind, not just the nation of Israel.

A 3-D miracle (6:16–24)

The inner circle of twelve men, the specially chosen followers of Jesus, have been spending intense time together. They've been able to observe how Jesus acts and reacts. They've seen some amazing things done, most recently the feeding from virtually nothing of a crowd that numbered around 20,000. But they can't quite figure Jesus out. Can this be the Messiah that their scriptures foretold? He doesn't seem to fit the image of the conquering king that they have imagined. And, despite all the hours they have spent together in close proximity, they are still not sure.

But then something happens that defies belief or explanation and gives them a clearer indication than they have ever had before of who this man really is. These are 3-D miracles: three different miracles dealing with three different dimensions.

The miracle of distance

There are a couple of geographic details which John's first readers would have picked up but which we miss out on. John has already told us that this all happened on and around the Sea of Galilee, and then adds in verse 15, 'Jesus, knowing that they intended to come and make him king by force, withdrew again to a mountain by himself.' Those who know the region will be aware that Jesus had gone up onto one of the high peaks that surround the northern area of Galilee.

But then some more detail is added. John tells us that the boat in which the disciples were travelling was about halfway across the sea, that is, about three and a half miles away from land, and that it was evening (a time when darkness had already fallen). Now, into that scene add the detail that Mark gives us in his account of what happened (Mark 6:46–48). Put together the clues. Jesus, who is up a mountain at least three and a half miles away from the disciples and in the darkness, *sees* the disciples 'straining at the oars'! Now that's a miracle!

The miracle of gravity

Jesus walked on water! And not just a few yards, but over three miles out into a deep and turbulent sea. Some of the great Jewish prophets and leaders of the past had parted water so that others could walk through on dry ground—people like Moses and Joshua—but none had ever defied gravity in this way and walked on top of water. The observable laws of science declare that this shouldn't happen. But Jesus did it! There's no other explanation than that this was an awesome miracle.

The miracle of space and time

The part that so many miss out is found in John's description in verse 21: 'Then they were willing to take [Jesus] into the boat, and *immediately* the boat reached the shore where they were heading.' Immediately! If these words are to be taken literally, then over three miles were travelled in an instant. A miracle that defied the observable laws of space and time! I think it's just as well it was dark—imagine what the sight of it would have done to the disciples!

John's concern throughout the Gospel is that we might share the disciples' experience and come to understand who this Jesus really was. And so John doesn't labour the astonishing nature of the miracles that have been performed. Rather he focuses our attention on the way Jesus made himself known to the disciples (vv. 19–20).

> John's concern throughout the Gospel is that we might share the disciples' experience and come to understand who this Jesus really was.

At first glance, it just seems to be a simple way of Jesus introducing himself to the disciples on the boat and calming their fears. A sort of 'Don't worry, it's only me'. But as we've discovered many times already in this Gospel, John is a master at hinting at the meaning below the surface. And the words Jesus uses here to identify himself could very legitimately be translated as 'I am': 'When they had rowed three or three and a half miles, they saw Jesus approaching the boat, walking on the water; and they were terrified. But he said to them, "*I am; don't be afraid*"' (vv. 19–20).

We need to realize that, to the Jewish mind, these were the very words that God used to introduce himself to Moses. These were God's special words. This was God's special description. (See Exod. 3:13–14.)

How was Jesus from Nazareth able to perform these

astounding, amazing, nature-controlling miracles? It was because he was God. This was no ordinary man. This man was none other than God in human flesh: fully man, fully God.

The bread of life (6:25–40)

Some commentators have divided up the three years of Christ's public ministry in this way: the first year, they call the year of inauguration, the second year, the year of popularity, and the third year, the year of opposition.

We are at that bridging point between the year of popularity and the year of opposition. We saw how the story of the feeding of the 5,000 men culminated in the desire of the people to make Jesus king by force. But now, following the miraculous walking on the water and the arrival of Jesus and his disciples at Capernaum, the tide begins to turn as Jesus teaches the people in the synagogue. And at the conclusion of this difficult and lengthy sermon we read, 'From this time many of his disciples turned back and no longer followed him' (v. 66).

In verses 25–40, we can see some of the reasons why people began to desert Jesus, and indeed, why people today will not follow him.

> The people following Jesus lived under a system that had become so corrupted as to suggest to them that religious performance was all that was needed to enjoy friendship with God.

Because they were religious

The people following Jesus lived under a system that had become so corrupted as to suggest to them that religious performance was all that was needed to enjoy friendship with God. These were people who attended church (v. 59) and who knew their Bible history and could quote the Bible (v. 31). And yet, these were people who walked away, rejecting Jesus Christ, God's special deliverer. They felt safe and content in their religious performance. What need did they have of Jesus?

Because they were more interested in material possessions than spiritual truth

The crowds were following Jesus because of what they could get out of him (vv. 26, 30–31). And it was as Jesus exposed their motives and revealed his spiritual mission that they began to disown him and drift away.

Because they could not understand grace

In verses 27–29, Jesus told them that God's salvation is a gift—'which the Son of Man will give you'—and that all that was required was to believe in what God had done for them. But they couldn't get their heads around this: 'What must *we do* to do the works God requires?'

Because they would not accept the evidence they had seen

The people in the crowd told Jesus they would believe in him as long as he performed an impressive miracle (vv. 30–31). But they had already witnessed, either first-hand or by immediate report, Jesus miraculously feeding around 20,000 near the north-eastern shore of Galilee, before they followed him to Capernaum (vv. 23–24). But they would not believe on Jesus, even after having witnessed such a stunning and significant miracle.

Because they did not recognize Jesus for who he was

There are at least four ways in which Jesus described himself
in the message he delivered:

- 'the Son of Man' (v. 27)
- 'the one [God] has sent' (v. 29)
- 'the bread of life' (v. 35)
- '[the one] come down from heaven' (v. 38).

Although we might struggle to understand the full
implication of these claims, his Jewish listeners didn't (vv.
41–42). Yet, despite all that had gone before, the harsh
reality of unbelief remained. They could not accept that
Jesus was the one he claimed to be.

Because they hadn't been chosen by God

The Bible teaches that God is in control of all things and
therefore he has chosen people to be his children—truths that
Jesus emphasizes in verse 37. 'Ah,' says someone, 'here's the
Bible teaching that there's only a few chosen people who will
become Christians, and I'm afraid that I'm not among those
who have been chosen by God. So what's the point of seeking
God?' But alongside that first truth there is also the teaching
that God's choice is gracious, lavish and generous. And the
balance between God's sovereign choice and his gracious
invitation is captured by Jesus in his words here: 'All that the
Father gives me will come to me, and *whoever comes to me I
will never drive away.*'

Feeding on Jesus (6:41–59)

What is it that shapes and affects who and how we are in

the totality of our being? We are so much more than just a combination of water and chemicals. We are not just shaped by automatic DNA responses or controlled by the electrical impulses that whizz through the synapses of the brain. No—we are shaped by all those influences and experiences that have gone into being a part of us. In the broadest sense, 'we are what we eat'.

That's the picture Jesus used when preaching to the Jews in the synagogue at Capernaum. He said, 'I'm the bread of life' (v. 35). He said, 'You need to eat me to live.' And for those who didn't understand the illustration but took him literally, this was a problem (v. 52). They failed to understand the metaphor that not only are you what you eat physically, but also you are what you eat spiritually. It is actually the latter that is more important than the former. It is far more important that we are well spiritually than that we are fit and healthy physically.

The reality is that, however carefully we might look after our bodies, they stop working. But the soul is immortal. We are made for eternity (vv. 57–58). Jesus was contrasting physical food with the spiritual sustenance that he could give. Food, such as the manna the Israelites ate when travelling to Palestine, couldn't stop them from dying. It kept them going for a while but it could not answer the problems of ageing, decay and death. Jesus, however, said that he had come to give eternal life (vv. 47–50). In fact, this particular truth is repeatedly emphasized in this chapter (vv. 40, 47, 51, 54, 58).

When we eat food, it becomes a part of us. For example, the calcium from the milk we drink is used to strengthen and build bones—it becomes an integral part of what we are. In the same way, when we receive Jesus as our Lord and Saviour, we are connected to him in a deep, inseparable way (v. 56: 'whoever eats ... *remains* in

> Just as starving people will hungrily devour food that is given to them, so lost and helpless sinners will hungrily, passionately, absolutely throw themselves upon the only Saviour.

me'), just as strongly as God the Father is connected to God the Son (the same word is found in 14:10: 'the Father, *living* in me'). We can never be parted. We are eternally secure.

So what is required in order to feed upon and enjoy all the blessings that Jesus, the bread of life, brings? What becomes clear is that when Jesus talks about feeding on him, it means the same as believing on him. Just as starving people will hungrily devour food that is given to them, so lost and helpless sinners will hungrily, passionately, absolutely throw themselves upon the only Saviour.

Reasons for rejection (6:60–71)

We began John 6 with a crowd of around 20,000 people; we end with just a dozen. Thousands of people had witnessed a stunning miracle; thousands of people had heard Jesus Christ speak. And thousands had rejected him and walked away.

In the first two years of Jesus's public ministry, he attracted a lot of attention, but large numbers began to leave him at this point in the story. These are the ones that John refers to as 'disciples' in verses 60–61 and 66. There were things that

Jesus was saying that they weren't prepared to think through (v. 60). They couldn't grasp the spiritual message (vv. 61–65). But the true disciples stayed (v. 67). They recognized Jesus for who he really was (v. 69). And once that had been grasped, little wonder they should ask, 'Lord, to whom shall we go?' For nothing compares to Christ.

However, Jesus knew that there was still one deceiver among the believers (vv. 70–71). The dangerous truth is that it is possible to think you are part of God's people when all along you are not. This was the tragedy of Judas.

The Feast of Tabernacles (7:1–13)

John had already dated this period for us by telling us it was around the time of the Jewish Passover (6:4), so when we come into chapter 7 and discover that another great Jewish festival—The Feast of Tabernacles—was about to begin, we realize that John has suddenly jumped a period of six months (Passover was in April, Tabernacles in October). Verse 1 summarizes events that fill six months and three chapters in Mark (chs. 7–9).

In verses 2–5 we discover Jesus's half-brothers urging him to take some action to restore his waning popularity. Elsewhere in the Gospels we are told that Mary had at least four sons by her husband Joseph: James and Jude (who were later to write two New Testament letters), and Joses and Simon. So it is likely that some, if not all, of these brothers came to speak to Jesus. They urged him to go with them down to Jerusalem for the Feast of Tabernacles and make some sort of public declaration that would attract a lot of publicity. This, they thought, would be his best chance of becoming someone famous and respected.

They urged him to make this trip to Jerusalem because people from all the towns and villages in Israel gathered there for this special Jewish feast. The only problem was that Jesus's own brothers did not believe in him (v. 5). He may have been a good brother, and they certainly had witnessed some of the miracles he had performed; but they could not believe that he was God's promised rescuer of the world, the long-awaited Messiah. He didn't fit the picture they had created. The Messiah was supposed to be a great military warrior, not the elder brother they had shared a room with. Maybe he could be a leading politician or rabbi (which was why they were happy to be his campaign managers), but there was no way he could be the Saviour of the world.

Little wonder, therefore, that Jesus responded as he did in verses 6–8 and left after his brothers so that he might remain secret during the first half of that eight-day-long celebration in Jerusalem (v. 10).

Jesus teaches at the feast (7:14–24)

Having delayed going from his home in Capernaum to Jerusalem for the annual Jewish Feast of Tabernacles, Jesus then appears in the area around the temple sanctuary and begins teaching the Jewish men who are gathered there. There is something about this teaching that amazes them (v. 15). Jesus is speaking as someone who has remarkable insight into what the Bible teaches, yet he has not attended any of the famous rabbinical schools of his day.

It would seem that Jesus didn't teach in the way that other

rabbis taught. They were always quoting case history. But Jesus came in and quoted no authority other than the Bible itself. He did this with such skill and persuasiveness that the people were amazed by his wisdom. But his critics also wondered what his authority was. On which precedent was he building?

And the answer that Jesus gave was both simple and profound (v. 16). He told them that his authority was none other than God himself. He didn't hide behind human teachers. He went straight to the source of all wisdom.

> Jesus didn't hide behind human teachers. He went straight to the source of all wisdom.

But there have been many teachers and charlatans down through the centuries who have argued that what they are saying is precisely what God has said, and that therefore everyone should obey them. So what gave Jesus the right to say what he did? How did he authenticate his claim?

The NIV doesn't bring out the strength of the original in verse 17. The ESV translates the first part of that verse more helpfully: '*If anyone's will is to do God's will*, he will know whether the teaching is from God ...' Jesus said that the reason why people do not believe him is not to do with their intellects, it is to do with their wills. The great obstacle to hearing, understanding and believing what Jesus is saying is not that you are too clever or too foolish, but that you have a basic flaw in your nature that predisposes you against God.

Jesus went on to unpack this teaching by pointing out

the difference between him and Jewish rabbis, scribes and religious teachers (v. 18). There were teachers who were keen to show off how much they knew and how cleverly they could manipulate the arguments put forward by rabbis of the past. And then there was Jesus, whose commitment was to glorify God rather than work for his own popularity and prestige.

To drive the argument home, Jesus then went on to show how these religious leaders would even change their laws to suit their own purposes (vv. 22–24). The last time Jesus was in Jerusalem he caused uproar by healing a sick man on the Sabbath, the Jewish day of rest. But Jesus pointed out that the religious leaders said that, in order to keep the law, a baby boy had to have his foreskin cut off eight days after birth, even if that meant performing this ceremony on the Sabbath. It didn't make sense. It was a hypocritical system designed to make them feel good about themselves. So little wonder that the Jewish leaders would not accept the things Jesus was saying. Their hearts, minds and wills were predisposed to reject those things that glorified God and were naturally inclined towards those things that glorified themselves.

Water from the Rock (7:25–52)

Jews all around the world still celebrate two important national festivals that go back centuries in their history: the Day of Atonement (Yom Kippur) and the Feast of Tabernacles. It was the second of these that we read Jesus attending about six months before his execution. It was an eight-day festival intended to celebrate the ingathering of the grape and olive harvest, but it had additional elements deliberately tagged on to remind the Israelites of certain truths about their nation's past.

For one thing, all the men were expected to live in booths they had made from sticks and branches. Even if you lived in Jerusalem itself, you were expected to erect such a dwelling on the roof of your house and sleep in it during the days of the festival. This was done to remind them of the time when the Israelites had wandered around in the wilderness, staying in tents, before they entered their ancestral homeland of Palestine. Additionally, as well as the regular sacrifices that took place in the temple compound, there was a daily procession from the temple down to the Gihon Spring. This was an essential water source for Jerusalem, and from it a priest would fill a gold jug and then walk back up to the temple, where he would pour the water out by the altar.

The point of this elaborate ritual was to remind the Israelites of the time when they were in the wilderness almost dying of thirst, and God provided water that came from a rock and was sufficient to quench the thirst of the whole community.

So at this special feast we discover strong reminders to all the people that God not only rescued people wandering in the wilderness in the past, but also that he could be trusted to do it again in the future. And it is at this point that John records the following: 'On the last and greatest day of the Feast, Jesus stood and said in a loud voice, "If anyone is thirsty, let him come to me and drink. Whoever believes in me, as the Scripture has said, streams of living water will flow from within him"' (vv. 37–38).

And just to make sure we don't overlook the significance

of this imagery, John clarifies this in verse 39. He points to the new, indwelling work that God's Holy Spirit was to begin at Pentecost. No wonder he tells us that many were attracted to Jesus. Jesus authenticated his claims to authority by acts of divine power (v. 31). Others recognized that he was the deliverer who had been promised by God (vv. 40–41). And even those sent to arrest him recognized that there was something unique about this Jesus (v. 46).

> Even those sent to arrest him recognized that there was something unique about this Jesus.

But this passage also explains why some would not come to Christ and drink and be satisfied. Some had bought into popular myths (v. 27)—the myth being that the Messiah would suddenly appear in the temple. There were those who misunderstood what he was saying (v. 35). There were those who made quick, unthinking assumptions (vv. 41–42)—they thought they knew where Jesus came from: the Galilee region. They hadn't bothered to discover that Jesus was actually born in Bethlehem in Judea. And there were those like the religious leaders, who were opposed simply because of their own self-interest (vv. 47–48).

Later additions? (7:53–8:11)

If you have a modern translation of the Bible, you'll notice that these verses are either ruled off from the rest of the text (as in the NIV), or that explanatory notes are given at the bottom of the page. This is because the evidence suggests that this passage was never an original part of John's Gospel nor accepted as part of the Scriptures.

This doesn't mean the incident didn't happen. It just means that we can't be sure of its authenticity and that it was possibly added by a later writer in an attempt to illustrate some topical point.

Party people (8:12–30)

People knew how to party in the Middle East—not in the sense that many understand it today in the West, but in the sense of having a good time among friends and family. This was an integral part of the annual Feast of Tabernacles.

Officially, the Feast was held as a celebration of God's goodness in providing another harvest of dates, grapes and figs, but there were a number of additional elements that made this a special time. For one thing, everyone in Israel who could do so was expected to attend. For another, as we have seen, they were expected to live in booths they had made themselves out of branches, sticks and leaves.

Then at night, when darkness had enveloped the city, the people would make their way into the temple area, and there, in what was known as the Women's Court, four huge lamps were lit. These were so large that it is reported that the wicks were made from the discarded linen robes that the priests wore. Apparently, the glow from these lamps could be seen throughout the city. Into that area came the temple musicians, and by the light of those huge lamps the people danced through the night, singing songs and praises, celebrating God's goodness in its many forms. It was the biggest and the best of all the parties in Israel.

It was in this area of the temple on the last day of the festival that Jesus made his astounding declaration, 'I am the light of the world. Whoever follows me will never walk in darkness, but will have the light of life' (v. 12). Set in the context of this feast, this claim had stunning significance to Christ's listeners.

Jesus was not only telling the Jews that he was God incarnate, he was also telling them that he was the promised rescuer who was to come and deliver his people, the one they were looking forward to and anticipating. However, there was something else that Jesus said that would have resonated with his listeners: 'Whoever follows me will never walk in darkness, *but will have the light of life.*' The expression 'the light of life' pictured life being lived to the full. It was the very opposite of death, lostness and darkness. It was an image of blessing, joy, clarity and purpose. In the context of the Jews partying under the blazing lamps in the temple, the invitation from Jesus grows even more wonderful.

He was not only God, the promised Messiah, but he was also the one who came to give his followers the greatest joy, the deepest contentment, the greatest blessing, the everlasting party. Any teaching about following Christ that implies real loss, boredom or gloom, has not grasped the wonders of grace, the joy of forgiveness, or the blessings of adoption into God's family.

However, the reaction of the Pharisees to Jesus's claim continued the same. They just didn't see it. 'Give us evidence,' they said. And in effect, Jesus told them that, if they were blind to spiritual things, there was no way they could grasp his claims. A blind man cannot see light.

Family blindness (8:31–41)

We so love the idea that we are free; that we can make our own decisions; that we are the masters of our souls. But that's not what Jesus taught (v. 34). We are not free; we are slaves. We are programmed to act in God-rejecting, God-dishonouring ways.

Notice what emerges about the people to whom Jesus was speaking.

- 'To the Jews who *had believed in him*, Jesus said ...' (v. 31). These weren't the Pharisees or religious leaders, whose opposition was well known. These were people seriously interested in Jesus.
- 'We ... have never been slaves of anyone' (v. 33). They were obviously not talking about political or economic slavery, for the Israelites had often been in captivity. They were clearly talking about the spiritual privileges they knew in hearing about the one true God.
- 'Abraham is our father' (v. 39). In other words, because they were physically descended from Abraham, they thought they were guaranteed special access to God.

They were offended when Jesus told them they were in slavery to sin. Their immediate reaction was to list the privileges they enjoyed. So, in verse 32, Jesus told his listeners that 'the truth will set you free'. And he then listed some of the components of the truth.

The first, in verse 34, has already been considered. It begins when we recognize there is a problem that we can't deal with. And more than that: that this failure is not just an occasional, minor aberration, but is the very fixed nature of our hearts and personalities. We are slaves to the principle of disobedience and dishonour.

Only once we have grasped that truth are we in a position to move on to the second truth that Jesus brought out (v. 36). We can't end this slavery on our own; there needs to be a deliverer. Jesus had already identified himself as 'the Son' and told his listeners what 'the Son' would do. In verse 28 he had clearly referred to the death he would die on a cross just six months later there in Jerusalem, when he would be lifted up to die.

Who are you? (8:42–59)

But not only was Jesus claiming remarkable things about himself, he was also saying some hard-hitting things about the religious leaders of the Jewish community. They thought they were righteous Jews, the protectors of Israel, those on a fast track to heaven. But Jesus pointed out three tell-tale signs about their behaviour.

They did not hear or understand what Jesus was saying

They thought they had a special hotline to God, but they were unable to hear God's clearest word (v. 43). They were proud of their heritage, and yet unable to recognize the very Messiah they were anticipating. They were highly religious, and yet could not understand God's greatest act of mercy.

They wanted to do away with Jesus

They thought that their behaviour was protecting the honour of God, that it was somehow a safeguard for his character.

But their actions showed them wanting to do away with the one who perfectly revealed God: the one of absolute purity, truth and grace (v. 40).

They lied

These Jews, proud possessors of the Ten Commandments, were confident they would never break the ninth command about not bearing false witness, yet they made untrue and vile accusations against Jesus (v. 48). They were not true about themselves, nor were they true about Jesus. Christ gave a startling summary of what that behaviour really meant (v. 44).

Having identified the nature of his opponents, Jesus then went on to deal with their question: 'Who are you really?' We see he had a passion to bring God glory (vv. 49–50). He was the unique, sinless one (v. 46). He was the only one who could say, 'I tell the truth' (v. 45).

What did his unique and glorious behaviour reveal about who he really was? The answer is that he claimed nothing less than equality with God (v. 58). For Jesus to say 'I am' means that he was clearly claiming to be one with God (see Exod. 3:13–14). And this was abundantly obvious to his hearers, because they picked up stones to kill him for this blasphemy.

So who was this Jesus?

For further study ▶

FOR FURTHER STUDY

1. Research how the imagery of a stormy sea is often used in the Old Testament to describe troubled and chaotic times.

2. Read Exodus 3:13–14 to see how God's name was repeatedly used by Jesus in John's Gospel.

3. Have a look at Zechariah 14:8 and Ezekiel 47:1–12. How do these passages help us to understand Christ's use of water imagery in John 7:37–38?

4. The theme of light was familiar to Jewish people. Have a look at Psalm 27:1; 76:4; 104:2; Zechariah 14:6–8; Isaiah 60:1–3, 19–20. Why is light such an appropriate image?

TO THINK ABOUT AND DISCUSS

1. The world rejects Jesus because it is so often focused on its own needs. How easily do we let our lives (individual and corporate) become shaped by the same agenda?

2. What is it about the teaching of Jesus that is deeply offensive today? How should we respond?

3. How can 'good' people be the 'slaves of sin'?

5 The opposition is confronted

(9:1–10:42)

At the end of chapter 8, we noticed that the religious leaders 'picked up stones to stone' Jesus. So it's no accident that at the start of this section we come across the account of Jesus dealing with a blind man. God deliberately planned this event, and John especially records it, so that we might notice the similarity between the blind man and the way the Jewish leaders were behaving.

Blind faith (9:1–12)

Just as the man in this passage is blind and unable to see Jesus, so the same applies to the Jewish leaders. They are blind—spiritually blind. They can't see Jesus for who he really is. So when Jesus comes along and tells everyone that they are more wicked than they can possibly imagine, yet more loved than they can ever dream, the Jewish leaders just don't get it; it goes right over their heads. They are blind to it; there is no room in their thinking for such a verdict.

There is a gut instinct within most people that you get what you deserve in this life. Good happens to the good, and bad happens to the bad. It's a way of thinking that is revealed by the disciples of Jesus when they come across this man who has been blind since birth (v. 2). The reasoning is obvious: there is something bad in this man's life, so it must be because he or his parents have done bad in the past. He is only getting what he deserves.

So as Jesus leaves the temple, the hub of religious life full of dignified and proud religious people who are rejecting him, the contrast can't be more extreme. By all accounts, the man deserves nothing. But what he experiences is grace. For no other reason than his own sovereign choice, Jesus decides to heal this man. It even seems that the blind man has not asked to be healed.

This is grace, and this is what offended religious people then and still offends them today. This is the core truth concerning salvation: it's not something earned or merited.

Notice how Jesus healed this man (v. 6). Why did he do it like this? Well, we really don't know, but what becomes clear is that Jesus didn't use the same method with all those he healed. Sometimes he touched them; sometimes he just spoke a word; sometimes he healed from a distance. The wonder of this variety was that it put the emphasis on the person who was doing the healing rather than on the method employed. Imagine if Jesus healed all the sick people by spitting on the ground, making mud and then applying it to the needy areas.

You can guess what some of the tele-evangelists would be doing today! There'd be a whole lot of spit, a whole lot of mud, and a whole lot of self-glorifying nonsense. No—the emphasis was kept on Christ, his word and his power.

Imagine the scene. You're blind. Someone comes up and puts warm mud on your eyes. And this man's voice then tells you to go to the Pool of Siloam and wash it off. For a blind person to get to that place it will mean a difficult walk, culminating in a series of rock steps leading down to the water's edge. So what would you do? Amazingly, the blind man obeyed and went! Maybe he had heard that it was Jesus and knew of his reputation as a healer. Maybe he felt something happen to his eyes, and so hurried off to remove the hardening mud. Or maybe there was an authority about this voice that demanded obedience. We don't know. But what we do know is this: he went; he obeyed; he ventured out in faith.

Uncomfortable evidence (9:13–34)

Jesus is a very serious threat to the religious authorities. He has suggested that favour with God is something that can't be earned by the efforts of sinners but can only be received by the grace of God. Why, if this is true, then even the tax collectors and moral failures can be forgiven! That is quite unacceptable to the religious hierarchy, so there is no way they are willing to accept that Jesus can heal a blind man. It's just that the evidence is so overwhelming that they have to find a way to discredit it.

They try to discredit it on theological grounds: Jesus has healed the man on the Sabbath, their special religious day, and that is against their rule book (v. 16). Others wonder whether there has been a switch; whether this man who can now see isn't actually the one who was born blind (vv. 18–23). They try to pressurize the witness (vv. 24–25). They finally try to discredit the witness on the grounds of their great learning (vv. 28–34).

Spiritual sight as well (9:35–41)

Jesus hears that the blind man has been evicted from the synagogue, and, by implication, from mainstream Jewish cultural life, so he goes looking for him and finds him. Can you imagine the comfort this would give to those first readers of John's history? It was written in about AD 85, at a time when many Christians from Jewish backgrounds were facing severe persecution and alienation; for them to know that Jesus understood and sympathized with their situation would have brought tremendous comfort.

We need to remember that this man had never before seen Jesus. The last time they met was when Jesus had put mud on his eyes and told him to go and wash it off at the Pool of Siloam. So it was perfectly natural that Jesus should introduce himself to the man, but notice the way he did it. Jesus asked him if he believed in 'the Son of Man'. This was an expression pregnant with meaning for Jews. From the Old Testament, they understood it to mean the promised one who would reveal God.

So, in effect, Jesus was inviting him to make the connection. He'd already enabled him to have physical sight; now the man revealed that he had spiritual sight as well, for he acknowledged that Jesus was indeed that divinely promised rescuer (v. 38). And he gave to Jesus the worship and honour that are his by right. Jesus not only fulfilled God's words, he also authenticated his authority through what he did and said. And the once-blind man saw it. He recognized what was obvious—that Jesus was the promised King. There was no blindness there.

But what about the religious leaders who had rejected Jesus? The final three verses of this passage bring the message home (vv. 39–41). When Jesus said that he had come 'for judgment', he was not contradicting his words in 3:17. Jesus came to rescue the lost and redeem the captives. But in revealing God's gracious plan of salvation, it was inevitable that he would expose the false ideas of those opposed to grace.

> In revealing God's gracious plan of salvation, it was inevitable that he would expose the false ideas of those opposed to grace.

Bad shepherds (10:1–10)

Jesus Christ loves and welcomes outsiders. That truth is declared throughout the pages of the Bible, and is made especially clear in John 10. To grasp this as fully as we ought, we need to make the connection with the previous chapter. Chapter 9 was about a blind man that Jesus healed, who was then thrown out of the synagogue by the religious leaders. Today, with our Western eyes, we can find it hard to grasp the profound impact that being thrown out of synagogue would have had, but the reality then was that the person became an outsider, rejected by his or her own community.

78

So we must understand that what we read about in John
10 is directly linked to the outsider in chapter 9. But there's
another thing we need to grasp before we try to understand
what Jesus is saying in these verses: not only was the sheep
imagery used here familiar to people who worked the land,
but it was also familiar to the Jews as a symbol that had
often been used in the Old Testament. In fact, there were
numerous occasions when the Israelites were referred to as
'sheep' and their leaders as 'shepherds'. Little wonder that
their greatest king, the one who acted as the model for all
the leaders that were to follow, was King David, who started
life as a shepherd and often saw life's journey through a
shepherd's eyes. And for those who were listening to Jesus,
it was inevitable that they should think of the famous words
that had been written in Ezekiel 34 about 600 years earlier
(see Ezek. 34:1–4, 11–12, 22–24).

It was common for Jewish villages to build a communal
sheep pen where the various shepherds who worked out of
that village could 'park' their sheep overnight. The shepherds
could then get a good night's sleep while a villager was
employed as the night watchman. When morning came, the
watchman would open the gate for the shepherds and they
would collect their flocks. But all these sheep from different
flocks were mixed together in this village sheep pen. How
would each shepherd know which of the sheep belonged
to him? Easy! He would call out each sheep by name. And
the sheep would recognize the voice and follow after the
shepherd.

It seems that, through using this imagery, Jesus was making
some pertinent comments. Firstly, there was criticism of the

religious leaders who had rejected him, were plotting his death and had expelled the healed blind man. These leaders were the thieves and robbers who had illegitimately got control of the sheep. But then, secondly, Jesus was identifying himself as God's promised shepherd leader (v. 11). Jesus will gather his own flock of sheep, who are known because they follow his call.

But it doesn't seem that the people grasped what he was saying (v. 6). (And we're not surprised, because we're told that some of them were Pharisees, the very group Jesus was criticizing.) So Jesus used some other sheep imagery (vv. 7–10). This isn't an allegory, in which every detail symbolically represents something else. Rather we have to grasp the big themes that Jesus was seeking to illustrate. It seems that Jesus moved from talking about the communal village sheep pen to the shelters that each shepherd constructed specifically for his own flock, and where the sheep would be sheltered during the intense afternoon heat. Some commentators point out that shepherds would often lie across the entrance to these pens, thus acting as human shields.

So, once again, we find criticism of the religious leaders, the 'thieves and robbers', who only want to 'steal and kill and destroy'. And again we find Jesus talking about the fact that he alone is able to provide for and protect the flock, only this time he changes the imagery from that of the shepherd who leads out his flock, to that of the gate of his flock's sheep pen. The added emphasis here is upon the safety, security and belonging that the flock experiences with Jesus, compared with those who are led by the destructive religious leaders of Israel and who experience only loss.

The good shepherd (10:11–21)

The religious leaders of the Jewish community exercised enormous control over their people. They ensured that the people conformed to the expected rules. They promised security and identity at a time of Roman occupation. The trouble was, they didn't really care for the people. They were in it for the money and the power. And when this startling new rabbi, Jesus, emerged out of Galilee performing miracles and calling the people to repent and prepare for judgement, they felt threatened, especially when, using sheep imagery, he criticized their leadership.

In this passage Jesus gives some tests to help distinguish the false leaders ('shepherds') of Israel from God's appointed King.

What are they like?

What is the nature of their characters? Jesus contrasts the character of the good shepherd with that of the other so-called leaders of his day (vv. 11–12). The word 'good' here doesn't mean weak or wimpish. In the original Greek, two words could be used to mean 'good'; here the far stronger of the two is employed. It means someone who is good and noble, pre-eminent and excellent. What a contrast to those Jewish leaders—the hired hands—who were only in it for the money and power, and were therefore willing to plot and cheat and conspire to murder.

How much do they care?

The difference in care between the good shepherd and the hired hand is most revealing. For the hired hand, it's only a job—they're not his sheep; whereas for Jesus, those sheep belong to him (v. 12). But more than that: he not only owns the sheep, he also knows them intimately and thoroughly (vv. 14–15). The expression here is of the deepest knowledge possible.

> Jesus not only owns the sheep, he also knows them intimately and thoroughly.

So what does Jesus, the good shepherd, do for the sheep he knows, owns and loves? The expression is used five times:

- 'The good shepherd lays down his life for the sheep' (v. 11)
- 'I lay down my life for the sheep' (v. 15)
- 'I lay down my life' (v. 17)
- 'I lay it down of my own accord' (v. 18)
- 'I have authority to lay it down' (v. 18).

How much does the good shepherd love his sheep? The bottom line is this: Jesus was willing to go to the cross and suffer in our place. Such is his love. Just in case some say that for God to die in that way was cheap—after all, he is the Creator—look at the word Jesus used in verse 11 to describe his life. He didn't use the Greek word *bios* (which referred to the physical side of life), and he didn't use the Greek word *zoe* (which referred to life's history); instead he used the Greek word *psuche*, which meant 'soul', the totality of his being, the essence of his life. This means that Jesus loves his sheep so much that he gave himself completely, utterly, totally for them.

What is their goal?

When discerning the worth of a leader, this question of purpose in leadership must be posed. Again, the good shepherd made this clear (v. 10). But Jesus was also assembling a flock of his own that was broader than the Jewish nation (v. 16). And this good news has travelled the globe.

Unsurprisingly, these words caused an immense furore. The Jewish leaders felt threatened and the religious zealots felt undermined, while poor, helpless failures rejoiced in the message of grace. And things were coming to a head. The division was emerging, the distinction becoming evident (vv. 19–21).

The nature of unbelief (10:22–26)

The time difference between verses 21 and 22 is about ten weeks. John tells us that Jesus came back down to Jerusalem to attend another of the special Jewish festivals, the Feast of Dedication. This feast celebrated how the Jews, under the leadership of Judas Maccabeus, had recaptured the temple and overthrown the occupying force that had been led by the Syrian Antiochus Epiphanes. We know this festival today by its more familiar name of Hanukkah. It had been decreed that celebrations should take place for eight days, beginning on 25 Kislev (which is the Jewish month that virtually corresponds to our December).

Hence John informs us that it was now winter, which helps us understand why in this cold, wet season, Jesus should be walking in the covered area of the temple known as Solomon's Colonnade. While he is there, he is surrounded by a number of Jews and confronted with a question. It is this occasion that leads to an exchange that makes even clearer the division recorded at the end of the last section.

Why do people not believe?

Because of false assumptions: 'If you are the Christ, tell us plainly' (v. 24)

Now why did they have to ask this? It was because Jesus had never explicitly said to them, 'I am the Messiah.' He had pointed at it in many other ways, but he had refrained from using that expression. And the reason he had done so was because his listeners understood 'Messiah' to mean someone who would come and exercise military and political power. And that was not what true Messiahship was about. That was not what Jesus had come to achieve. So little wonder that, at this feast that celebrated a military victory over a foreign overlord, Jesus should refuse to fit into their wrong categories and accommodate himself to their false assumptions.

Because of poor listening: 'I did tell you, but you do not believe' (v. 25)

There's a difference between not being able to understand (because of those false assumptions) and not being willing to listen. Jesus was crystal clear in what he was pointing to; it was just that there was a complete lack of willingness to hear the things he was saying. They conflicted so sharply with all the Jews had prided themselves upon.

Because of bad sight: 'The miracles I do in my Father's name speak for me' (v. 25)

Not only could the Jews not hear or understand what Jesus was saying, they couldn't see the evidence that was before them. Jesus had confirmed his claims time after time, miracle after miracle. But still they couldn't see.

Because of the wrong owner: 'you do not believe because you are not my sheep' (v. 26)

This is startling. To many, it is offensive. Jesus was telling his listeners that he had not called them. They did not belong to his flock. So it was no surprise that they should react with unbelief. And the reality is this: you can't come to God unless God calls you.

Why do people believe?

Because of attentive hearing: 'My sheep listen to my voice' (v. 27)

How do you know if someone is a real Christian? Because he or she is drawn to the words of Jesus, there is a love for the Scriptures and there is attentiveness to the ministry of the Word. For the believer knows not only that these words are always true, but also that they are relevant and shaping; that they lead into joy and peace.

> A true believer in Jesus Christ has a sense of belonging, a sense of relationship.

Because of the true shepherd: 'I know them' (v. 27)

A true believer in Jesus Christ

has a sense of belonging, a sense of relationship. Believers know that Jesus is fully aware of every part of them—sins and failures as well—and yet loves them graciously and unconditionally.

Because of clear vision: 'they follow me' (v. 27)

A real Christian is someone who obeys what Jesus says; someone who keeps his or her eyes on his example; someone who does what he commands. The bottom line is that the real believer has a new attitude that means God's will is no longer an obstacle but a privilege. The genuine Christian has a new agenda that puts God on top.

Because of genuine experience: 'I give them eternal life' (v. 28)

Something happens to those who entrust themselves to Jesus Christ. They are not given a straitjacket or confined to a joy-numbing, brain-destroying existence. Instead, they are given life to the full; a life with God that will never end.

Securely saved (10:27–42)

Jesus continued to use picture language, describing his followers as a flock of sheep (vv. 27–30). Christ's relationship with his people is infinitely strong. We noticed from verses 14–15 that his knowledge of his followers is as thorough and intimate as that which exists between the three persons of the Godhead. And yet he immediately went on to say that he was going to lay down his life for those people, despite all the sin, failure, compromise and weakness that was evident within them.

Christ's love for his people is seen not only explicitly in

these verses, but also implicitly in verse 29. There is an alternative reading to the first part of the verse because some of the early manuscripts have a minor variation, which many scholars claim has stronger textual support. That would mean translating verse 29 as follows: '*What my Father has given me is greater than all*; no one can snatch them out of my Father's hand.' Jesus was declaring how precious his people really are to him. They are 'greater than all'. This is how he regards his flock.

Some people get the idea that the Christian faith is about something that happened in the past—Jesus dying on a cross—so that something might happen in the future—Christians going to heaven. And what they miss out is the part in-between, in the here and now. They see little relevance or impact in the Christian message for today. And yet what Jesus revealed in this whole 'shepherd' passage is that his care, love and oversight of the flock is something that is ongoing.

We noticed this back in verse 10: 'I have come that they may have life, and have it to the full.' And we discover that this same theme is implicit here. Unfortunately, the English language doesn't contain all the tenses that you find in New Testament Greek, because when we come to verse 28—'I give them eternal life' (which suggests that this is something that happens at a single point for the believer)—we discover that the Greek present indicative translated 'I give' indicates a continuous sense (or aspect). So a more literal translation would be 'I keep on giving to them eternal life'.

Christ's involvement with his people is continuous. Moment by moment, second by second, he is at work giving real, satisfying, eternal life. In fact, the 'shepherd' imagery fits perfectly. It reminds us that Jesus looks after his people in the same way the careful shepherd looks after his own flock, constantly on the lookout, not only for fresh pastures, but also for dangerous enemies.

In verse 12 Jesus said that wolves would attack his flock, and the word he used for 'attack' there is the same word that is translated 'snatch' in verse 28: 'no one can *snatch* them out of my hand.' So Jesus was saying that part of this living relationship his people have with him is that he will protect them from the attacks that will come. None of these attacks will be destructive. None of them will prise his people away from the flock. The attacks may hurt; his people may get bruised and battered. But Jesus will never let Satan's attacks overpower his people.

These verses contain one of the most glorious truths in the Bible: that those who belong to Jesus Christ can never, ever be lost. They will most certainly go to be with him in glory for time without end. Three reasons are given in this passage.

A strong word

Jesus said, 'I give them eternal life' (v. 28). The word translated 'eternal' is *aionios*, which occurs over sixty-five times in the New Testament and is used to describe the 'eternal' God. So you can see it is the strongest word that could be used to describe 'without end'.

A strong promise

Jesus went on to say, 'and they shall never perish'. But once again, the translation doesn't do justice to the original.

Literally it reads, 'they will indeed not ever perish'. It is an especially strengthened expression. You couldn't emphasize it more in the Greek if you tried. God's people may struggle, hurt, and go through times of dark, deep depression and of doubt and despair—but they can never perish.

A strong Saviour

It gets even better. It gets personal: 'no one can snatch them out of my hand.' And then to underline the meaning, a verse later, Jesus said, 'no one can snatch them out of my Father's hand.' And just to make sure that they noted the implication of what he had said, Jesus added, 'I and the Father are one.' And they got it, all right; they understood what Jesus was saying. They picked up stones to stone him to death, because (as they said in v. 33) 'you, a mere man, claim to be God'.

FOR FURTHER STUDY

1. Research how the theme of blindness is used within the book of Isaiah.

2. Where in the Bible is the title 'Son of man' used? Who does it describe?

3. Read Ezekiel 34:1–4, 11–12, 22–24. Why was this shepherding metaphor so associated with the kings of Israel?

TO THINK ABOUT AND DISCUSS

1. If people are spiritually blind, can they come to see God? If so, how?

2. What is it about the shepherd imagery that makes it such a good illustration of leadership?

3. What gives you the greatest assurance that you belong to Jesus?

6 Uncomfortable evidence

(11:1–54)

This is a pivotal section in John's account. He outlines a remarkable miracle (yet another 'sign') that forced the issues with the Jewish authorities and put them in an untenable position. They had to make a decision as to what to do with Jesus; they couldn't ignore him any longer. But John also uses this section to teach that the work of Jesus through death is to bring life!

A timely intervention (11:1–16)

John doesn't specifically identify where Jesus was staying at the time he received the news of Lazarus's illness; obviously, the length of journey that Jesus had to make to get to Bethany has an impact on some of the lessons we learn from this passage.

What John does tell us in 10:40 was that Jesus had gone

from Jerusalem 'across the Jordan to the place where John had been baptising in the early days'. But when we read 1:28 we find: 'This all happened at Bethany on the other side of the Jordan, where John was baptising.'

So there were two places that had the name Bethany. The trouble is that there is no known Bethany on the east bank, so some commentators have looked around, seen a place called Bethabara, just one day's journey away, and assumed that was the place being referred to. However, there is better justification for assuming that where Jesus stayed was actually 150 km away in a region called Batanea, which in Aramaic paraphrases can almost be spelt the same as 'Bethany'. And the journey from Batanea would have taken four days.

This is important information. It helps us work out the timing of events. A messenger is sent from Bethany when Lazarus is seriously ill. He arrives four days later in Batanea and tells Jesus. At that time it seems that Lazarus is still alive (v. 4). However, two days later, Jesus supernaturally knows that Lazarus has died. And so Jesus and the disciples set off on their four-day journey, arriving in Bethany to be told that Lazarus has been in the tomb for four days—which all ties in neatly together.

However, the question must be asked: Why did Jesus delay? Why did he not set off immediately for Bethany to visit the home of his friends? Yes, Lazarus would still have been dead for two days by our reckoning, but why the postponement of the trip? There was a superstitious Jewish belief at that time that the soul of a deceased person hovered over the corpse for three days until decomposition set in. In other words, it was not until the third day that death was considered to be irreversible.

Jesus made this statement while in Batanea about what was happening to Lazarus: 'it is for God's glory so that God's Son may be glorified through it' (v. 4). Now, we must be clear that Jesus was not saying he wanted to perform this amazing miracle so people would applaud and praise him, but rather so that men and women might have a clearer understanding of who he really was and therefore be able to trust him all the more. That is what was meant by him being 'glorified'—he was glorified when his character was made known.

The NIV translation gets the connection between verses 5 and 6 badly wrong: 'Jesus loved Martha and her sister and Lazarus. *Yet* when he heard that Lazarus was sick, he stayed where he was two more days.' This suggests a contrast or disconnection between Jesus's love for the family and how he acted. But when you translate the Greek text literally, it reads like this: 'Jesus loved Martha and her sister and Lazarus. *Therefore* when he heard that Lazarus was sick, he stayed where he was two more days.'

So there is not a contrast or disconnection; quite the opposite. The text makes clear that there is a continuation between how Jesus loved the family and how he acted. It was because of, not despite, his love for them that he waited two days. This reinforces the big-picture teaching of the Bible that God is in control and that he

> God knows what he is doing when he delays. He has his glorious purposes and they are all bound up with Jesus being known and trusted.

loves his children more than they can ever understand. This means that God knows what he is doing when he delays. He has his glorious purposes and they are all bound up with Jesus being known and trusted.

Life lessons (11:17–37)

For the sisters from Bethany, their grief was still raw. Lazarus had only been dead for four days. And such was the respect in which they were held that many had come from nearby Jerusalem to try to bring comfort. But there was one the sisters wanted to see more than anyone else. It was their dear friend, Jesus of Nazareth. They'd sent a message to him ten days before, but he had been delayed. But now word had come through that he was just arriving. And so Martha, the impetuous and busy sister, immediately rushed out of the family home to meet him. And the first thing she said to him was to do with the 'what if's that she and Mary had obviously talked about (v. 21). She had seen Jesus perform amazing miracles. He'd healed all kinds of sick people. Only a few months previously he had restored sight to a blind man. So she and Mary were sure that, if only Jesus had been nearby when Lazarus fell sick, he could have healed him also. But he hadn't been. And Lazarus was now dead.

She wanted Jesus to know that they still had confidence in him (v. 22). Now, this wasn't Martha trying to persuade Jesus to raise Lazarus from the dead, for it is clear from verse 39 that she wasn't expecting any such thing. Rather it was just her affirmation of ongoing trust in what Jesus was about. And the response of Jesus to her sounded just like the sort of well-worn phrase that we roll out on such difficult occasions (v. 23), to which Martha replied with what sounded like the usual response (v. 24). Martha was a good Jewess. She believed that there was something after death. The Scriptures made this clear (even though one section of the Jewish religious elite—the Sadducees—were now saying that this was nonsense and that death was the end). But Martha, along with thousands of her fellow citizens, had this general feeling that it wasn't the end, that there was more, that there was some sort of life after death.

Notice how Jesus took that general, orthodox response of Martha's and clarified it with a stunning, specific claim (vv. 25–26). He was saying that it is not enough to have a general idea of life after death; rather, if you want to experience it, you must have a specific belief in him—the only one who can provide it. He is the one who gives that life.

This is the fifth time in John's Gospel that Jesus has used that expression 'I am', which, as we have seen, is a declaration of great and revealing importance. On each of those occasions Jesus had been using a picture or teaching from Israel's past and showing how it was a pointer to him; that he was the fulfilment of what they were speaking about. Here Jesus took up the Old Testament teaching about resurrection and said that it found its perfect fulfilment and completion in him.

Jesus put it in two ways:

Firstly, he said, 'He who believes in me *will live, even though he dies.*' In other words, the person who has put his or her complete trust in the person and work of Jesus Christ will experience, after death, that new and eternal life that Jesus promised. Secondly, Jesus developed this by saying, 'and whoever lives and believes in me *will never die.*' The abundant life that Jesus promised doesn't start when we die. It starts now. It starts when we trust him. Death will be that momentary interruption as we move from the earthly scene to the heavenly one. In that sense, as Jesus said, we will never die. The real life will never end.

And what is the condition? 'I am the resurrection and the life. He who *believes in me* will live, even though he dies; and whoever lives and *believes in me* will never die. *Do you believe this?*' It doesn't require religious ceremonies or hard work; all that is required is faith in Jesus Christ.

> The abundant life that Jesus promised doesn't start when we die. It starts now. It starts when we trust him.

Martha had grasped it. When Jesus asked her whether she believed, she responded with one of the greatest and most confident affirmations in Scripture. '"Yes, Lord," she told him, "I believe that you are the Christ, the Son of God, who was to come into the world."' She knew who he was—the unique rescuer sent from God; the one who had been promised down through the centuries to deal with his people's sin and failure.

The life-giver (11:38–44)

In accordance with local custom, Lazarus would have been buried within twenty-four hours of his death. But Middle Eastern funeral customs meant that this wasn't cremation or being placed in a hole in the ground. Rather, as was common among the Jews, the dead were buried in caves—whether man-made or natural. And in those caves they would construct or carve out a little room or chamber in which the body would be laid, wrapped in a linen sheet, the head covered with another cloth. A stone was then rolled over the mouth of the cave to keep out stray animals and keep in vile odours. The plan was that one year after the death the family would return to the burial chamber and recover the bones (from which the flesh had by now rotted away) and store those bones in a little box that would be kept in a hole in the wall of the outer burial chamber.

We noted in the 'Background and Summary' chapter John's purpose in writing. In this account, these elements are clearly seen together.

He provides evidence of what Jesus did

It doesn't get much bigger than this. All through his Gospel John has been recording remarkable miracles that Jesus performed—turning water into wine, healing the official's sick son, restoring a cripple, feeding 5,000, walking on water and giving a blind man his sight. But here is the climactic miracle of his earthly ministry—he raised the dead. And not someone who had just passed away, but someone whose body had begun to decay and putrefy. John records the details for us with dramatic precision (vv. 43–44).

What an astounding miracle! This wasn't something that John could fabricate. This wasn't done in an unknown village in the middle of nowhere—this was Bethany, just outside the capital city of Jerusalem. Little wonder that John was to record the following a chapter later: 'Now the crowd that was with him when he called Lazarus from the tomb and raised him from the dead continued to spread the word.

Many people, because they had heard that he had given this miraculous sign, went out to meet him' (12:17–18). Here was evidence that could be checked out. This was an account that could bear the closest scrutiny and examination.

He points to who Jesus is

John doesn't want us to be left gawping at the miracle without grasping who it was who performed it. He wants us to understand some vital and basic truths about Jesus Christ.

For one thing, he reminds us of the love of Jesus for sin-sick and sorrowing people (vv. 32–38). Here is one who is not distant and far removed, but who understands, loves and knows what it is to experience heart-wrenching pain.

In this section we come to a prayer of Jesus's that has confused many (vv. 41–42). In fact, what Jesus was doing before he raised dead Lazarus was to show the people that he acted in absolute reliance on and total obedience to God the Father.

He prompts faith in what Jesus promises

It's not enough just to enjoy these historical accounts or simply to grasp certain facts about who Jesus is; it must lead to a response. As John says, '... these are written that you may believe that Jesus is the Christ, the Son of God.' The only appropriate response to these truths is to believe; to trust Jesus (vv. 39–41). This was the outcome for many of those who had come from Jerusalem to pay their respects to the family and then witnessed what Jesus did (v. 45).

Bury the evidence (11:45–54)

What do you do when the evidence is against you? This was a problem facing the ruling Jewish party. They had come to an understanding with the occupying Roman forces that they could control considerable money-making schemes and enjoy a position of power and leadership within their own community. But for that to continue, they needed to ensure that there were no problems, that the Romans weren't aggravated and that the people placidly accepted the status quo.

But a serious problem had arisen. There was a teacher who had been moving around Israel for the previous three years and was causing great unrest. Nationalistic expectations were rising and there was the danger that there could be a rebellion against the occupying forces. And to cap it all, this Jesus had just performed the most amazing miracle that anyone could think of. He had raised to life someone who had been dead for four days. And he had done this in a village that was next to Jerusalem, the capital, so they couldn't discredit the miracle in any way. Many from Jerusalem had actually seen him do it, and many could pop over to this village to see this undead man for themselves (vv. 45–48). But rather than stop and think and consider the evidence that was there before their eyes, the gut instinct of these religious leaders was to protect what they had. The trouble was, they couldn't ignore what was happening. They needed a course of action, and their leader, Joseph Caiaphas, who had been high priest for about a dozen years, came up with a suggestion that was more perceptive and profound than he could ever have imagined (vv. 49–50).

This was not driven by high motives. He said, 'it is better for *you* that one man die.' He wasn't talking about the good of the nation or the safety of the people. The Greek makes it plain that he was talking about the self-interest of the Jewish ruling party. In the Greek, the phrase 'that one man die for the people' would have reminded them of the sacrifices they offered at the temple in Jerusalem. The basis for these sacrifices was substitution: one died in place of another. An animal was sacrificed to take the guilt of another. A scapegoat was sacrificed and another freed as a picture of someone dying in the place and for the sake of another. And this is exactly the imagery that Caiaphas used. Let Jesus die so we can carry on.

John saw the irony and significance of what Caiaphas said. Caiaphas had meant it in only a very limited way, but John recognized that the death of Jesus was going to be a substitution of far greater significance. So he deliberately highlights this for us (vv. 51–52). 'Yes,' says John, 'you are more right than you know, Caiaphas. Jesus is going to die in the place and for the sake of others, but it will be for all of God's people everywhere.'

For further study ▶

FOR FURTHER STUDY

1. Research how death is bound up with judgement in the Old Testament (see, for example, 1 Sam. 25:38; 2 Sam. 6:7; Acts 12:23). How does this help us further understand the work of Christ on the cross?

2. Research how the principle of substitution is found in the Jewish sacrificial system (start, perhaps, with Lev. 16). Where else in his Gospel has John hinted at the fact that Jesus is the substitute for others?

TO THINK ABOUT AND DISCUSS

1. Can you think of occasions when God has delayed giving an answer to you, but later on you have understood how God was glorified through the delay?

2. Why did Jesus weep (11:35)? What comfort can we take from this verse?

3. What do you think will happen to you when you die? Why? How do you feel about this?

7 A week of preparation

(11:55–12:50)

Passover was one of the most important religious festivals for Jews. It was the time when they remembered how they had escaped from slavery in Egypt. And how did that happen? A lamb was sacrificed. And every Passover they would kill and eat a lamb to remember that event. So the theme of Jesus dying for others as the Lamb of God is highlighted again through this festival.

Preparing for burial (11:55–12:11)

As we read these verses, we also pick up on the theme of burial. Jesus said the reason why Mary anointed him with expensive and pungent perfume (12:3) was in anticipation of his death and burial. We don't know how aware Mary was of the significance of what she was doing, but it does seem that, as one who listened carefully to Jesus, she had a sense of his impending death and wanted to show her love and gratitude while he was still alive.

It is clear that everything was building towards this climax when Jesus would die—not by accident but as the culmination of God's rescue plan. But when we come to study a Bible passage, we should look out not only for how it develops themes, but also for how it highlights significant contrasts. And in the incident of the anointing there are a couple of contrasts John wants us to notice.

Firstly, he draws our attention to the fact that Lazarus was present at this meal in Bethany that had been given in honour of Jesus. So we have sitting here the man who was dead but now is alive, as well as the man who is alive but will soon be dead. The second contrast is between the other two principal characters—Mary and Judas. Mary is the one who lavishly gives in love to Jesus. We are told that this perfume was worth a year's wages (12:5) and that Mary emptied it on Jesus and then loosened her hair and wiped his feet with it. What a stunning image of love and commitment! But then there is Judas. Selfish Judas. Judas the thief. Judas who cared about his religious image and talked about giving money to the poor when all he really thought about was himself. Judas who was willing to criticize others. Judas who didn't have a gracious word (12:5–6). What a contrast! What a difference between these characters! And that is precisely what John wants us to see, because it highlights the contrast between those who love Jesus and those who still continue in their sin.

John includes some details in his Gospel that make us realize we are listening to eyewitness accounts. John remembers the effects of Mary's action; it is as if he can still smell the strong fragrance in his nostrils (12:3). But what about Judas—what were the consequences for him? John waits a few chapters to tell us, but Matthew and Mark add a significant detail in their accounts (Matt. 26:14–16; Mark 14:10–11).

The entry of the Messiah (12:12–19)

The Jewish people were fiercely independent and had a history of uprisings and revolts to throw out foreign rulers. And now, packed into Jerusalem and surrounding areas was a crowd of about 2.5 million people, 2 million of whom had left their homes to be present in Jerusalem for the Passover festival. So the atmosphere was white-hot with expectation. And, to cap it all, everyone was talking about this new teacher from Galilee who had been performing some incredible miracles. Could he be the rescuer that God had promised their nation? Could this be the time when the revolt would begin and the Roman forces be evicted?

And then the cry went up, 'He's coming!' A great crowd of pilgrims streamed out of the city to greet him, and they were met by a great crowd of people who were accompanying this Jesus from where he had been staying in Bethany. And as the crowds converged, the excitement was tangible, the expectations sky high.

So what did the crowd do? They waved palm branches. Why palm branches? Because palm branches had become the symbol of Jewish nationalism. Palm branches were waved when a previous Jewish fighter, Simon the Maccabee, had driven out occupying Syrian forces. In other words, palm branches were to do with nationalist hope, revealing that the crowd believed that Jesus was going to be the deliverer who would eject the Romans.

Listen to the songs they sang and the words they used.

'Hosanna'

This wasn't an empty expression. It literally meant 'save us now'. And in the context of what was happening, the 'save us now' had clear reference to salvation from the Roman occupation.

'Blessed is he who comes in the name of the Lord!'

This was taken from Psalm 118, a hymn that was sung in the temple every morning and which the Jews understood to refer to the coming Messiah who would rescue his people. So the crowd identified Jesus as the conquering hero they had been looking for over the years. And just so we don't miss the point, they added, 'Blessed is the King of Israel!', which is not a quote from any part of the Bible but a clear pointer that they regarded the one 'who comes in the name of the Lord' as the king who would deliver his people.

Not only did the crowd wrongly assume that Jesus came to be a political deliverer, it would seem that the disciples thought that as well. At first, they didn't understand why Jesus had chosen to ride into Jerusalem on a donkey, when a white stallion would have been far more appropriate for a military general. It was only later that they realized that Jesus was doing precisely what God had planned should happen. Then they remembered the words from Zechariah 9:9 which had pointed to this mode of entry: 'See, your king comes to you … gentle and riding on a donkey, on a colt, the foal of a donkey.'

It was an excited crowd that accompanied Jesus into Jerusalem, and it was quite clearly a huge crowd as well. There were the people already in Jerusalem for the festival; the crowd coming in from Bethany; those who believed he could be the Messiah; and those who were just plain curious to see the man who had healed Lazarus. Little wonder the Pharisees' response to all of this was to complain (v. 19). What was their problem? What worried them was that more and more people were listening to what Jesus taught about the way to God rather than following their own strict code of rules and regulations.

We see John's deliberate irony as he records the Pharisees' statement that 'the whole world has gone after him!' They were referring to the crowds of Jewish people, but John saw the literal truth in that statement. Because Jesus was to die on that cross, all hopeless, law-breaking failures from everywhere on the face of this planet—and not just the adherents of strict Judaism—could be forgiven and made new. The Pharisees wanted to imprison people within their own code of religion. Jesus, out of amazing love, came to set people free who couldn't begin to follow that self-defeating rule book. He came to save hopeless people.

> The Pharisees wanted to imprison people within their own code of religion. Jesus, out of amazing love, came to set people free who couldn't begin to follow that self-defeating rule book.

Death for the world (12:20–36)

John often recorded times when Jesus told his followers that they weren't there yet: that the time for his climactic work had not yet arrived. Now in John 12 we come across these immensely significant words in verse 23: 'Jesus replied, "*The hour has come* for the Son of Man to be glorified."' It was here! The time had arrived!

John records how there were some Greeks in Jerusalem at that time who may well have been encouraged by the fact that Jesus was speaking of a salvation that didn't exclude them. They couldn't get close to the Holy Place in the temple because they were Gentiles, confined to one of the outer courts, but here was this remarkable leader speaking of God's plan for them. And so they asked Philip the disciple to arrange for them to see Jesus. It is significant that Jesus *didn't* meet with them. Instead he said, 'The hour has come for the Son of Man to be glorified.' In other words, Jesus was about to do something that would make it possible for all people, irrespective of national or cultural background, to have fellowship with God. And what was that thing?

Jesus immediately went on to talk about his death, which, he said, would make it possible for many people to find real forgiveness and real life (v. 24). Most of those listening worked the land and knew what he was talking about. You put a dead seed in the earth and, after a while, you have a harvest as that seed sprouts and produces many more. In the same way, Jesus told them, his death would produce a harvest of souls, which would include the likes of those Greeks who had been previously excluded.

The question arises: Why? Why did Jesus have to come? Why did he have to die? The answer comes in Jesus's description of how people really operate (vv. 25–26). Jesus was using a figure of speech that was common in that region. He was describing the choice that we all have to make— whether our passion is for what we can get out of this life for ourselves ('The man who loves his life') or to live under God's rule ('the man who hates his life in this world'). He wasn't using the words 'love' and 'hate' in their absolute sense, but rather as a form of speech indicating what our preferences are.

What Jesus was going to do wasn't going to be cheap. To rescue and redeem lost failures was going to take Jesus to a cross. He was going to be executed by the Romans in one of the cruellest deaths known to man. A Jew was normally stoned to death by his own community but Jesus knew that a different form of death lay ahead for him (vv. 32–33). Little wonder, then, that as he began to contemplate what lay ahead, he was troubled (vv. 27–28a). What lay ahead was the pain of betrayal and loneliness; the hurt of lies and injustice; the agony of torture and execution; and the greatest agony of all—that of bearing God's wrath for the sins of his people.

God's eternal justice was going to be vindicated (vv. 31–32). No one would ever be able to say that God turned a blind eye to sin and rebellion. The cross was the great revelation that God hates sin and must deal with it severely. The cross also dealt an eternally devastating blow to the one who had controlled, cheated and conned the lives of people down through the ages. The King was coming, and there on the cross he would break the power of sin and fear that Satan had used to imprison the world (Rom. 3:25b–26).

> The offer of salvation is conditional. It is time-limited. There will be a time when God will no longer challenge.

The offer of salvation is conditional. It is time-limited. There will be a time when God will no longer challenge; a time when his voice of grace and mercy will have grown silent (vv. 35–36). Notice what Jesus did, having spoken to them. He acted out his words. He gave them an object lesson of what he had said: 'When he had finished speaking, Jesus left and hid himself from them.' There can be nothing more terrifying than not being able to find Jesus; nothing to fear more than him hiding his grace and mercy from view.

Sight for blind eyes (12:37–50)

We have seen that the whole theme of belief is central to John's purposes in writing. Yet the reality was that most of the Jews who heard and saw Jesus did not put their trust in him. So as John summarizes Christ's three years of public ministry, he inevitably has to record the fact that the overwhelming majority did not believe in Jesus. How could this be? If Jesus was who he claimed to be, then why was God not granting success? Surely divine favour was sufficient to gain a following.

You can sense the exasperation and wonder in what John writes in verse 37. He makes clear that there were many other miracles that Jesus performed in addition to the awesome ones he has recorded. Yet despite what the people had seen and witnessed, the vast majority still did not believe that Jesus was God's promised rescuer. It wasn't as if these things had happened elsewhere. It wasn't as if they'd only read about them. These miraculous signs were actually performed 'in their presence'.

John says that God actually hardens the hearts of those who do not believe (vv. 39–40). That's shocking—and at first sight very confusing. Verse 39 begins with 'For this reason they could not believe'. What was this reason? We have to go back to verse 37: that 'they still would not believe in him'. So God hardens the hearts of those who deliberately refuse to believe in Jesus Christ. It's as if God's judgement upon sin is not just held back until later, but his immediate judgement upon unbelief is to harden the heart further. It's as if God allows sin to run its course—for sin naturally has a deadening effect. But alongside this truth we need to remember that the God who sovereignly hardens hearts is also the God who sovereignly intervenes and rescues. Indeed, as the quotations from Isaiah reveal, God uses hardened hearts for his glory and purpose in rescuing the lost and exalting his name.

Just as John summarizes the response to Christ's earthly ministry in these verses, he also summarizes the message that Jesus declared.

When you believe in Jesus, it means you recognize that Jesus Christ is none other than God in human flesh—the one who is eternally divine and fully human at one and the same time (vv. 44–45). That means Jesus was so much more than just a good example, a wonderful teacher, a miracle worker or a great philosopher. It means that Jesus was uniquely

God's gracious rescue plan. If you want to know what God is like, look at Jesus. John has already illustrated this truth in a stunning way. In verse 40 he quoted from Isaiah 6:10. What was Isaiah 6 about? It was the time when Isaiah was given an amazing vision of God (Isa. 6:1–3).

So here we have this remarkable, awe-inspiring vision of Yahweh God. Now look at what John goes on to say in verse 41. It doesn't come much clearer than this. We must believe that Jesus fully reveals God.

Jesus came into this world not only to reveal God, but primarily to carry out God's rescue plan (vv. 46–47). This world is held captive in the darkness of sin, but Jesus came to save men and women from all over the face of this planet. And what is the condition of salvation? That we 'believe in me'.

We must not imagine that somehow we can sneak into heaven by another route; that somehow our sins will be conveniently forgotten or swept under the carpet. Jesus declared that we will be judged according to what we have heard (v. 48). And the Bible suggests that this standard remains—that those who have heard the free offer of salvation through faith in Christ will be judged all the more severely if they reject it. There was a unique authority about the teaching of Jesus, for he was reporting not his own thoughts but the very words of God (vv. 49–50). He issued the clear commands of the Commander-in-Chief. As Jesus tells us, 'his command leads to eternal life.'

1. Find where in this Gospel John has used the expression 'the hour'/'the time' (or its equivalent). What does each refer to?

2. Read Zechariah 9:9–13. How did the crowd on the first Palm Sunday misinterpret this passage?

3. Look at Isaiah 6:1–3. Why was John able to say what he did about this passage in 12:41?

4. Identify the parts of John 12 that deal with the theme of Christ's death for all the world.

TO THINK ABOUT AND DISCUSS

1. Many wanted Jesus to fulfil their own (nationalistic) agenda. How might we 'use' Jesus for our own purposes today—individually? As churches? Nationally?

2. How was God the Father glorified through the death of Jesus? What are the implications for us?

3. Some people do not confess their faith for fear of what others may think. Have you ever been like this? How can this fear be overcome?

8 Preparing the disciples

(13:1–14:31)

The Christian message turns the world's way of thinking on its head. Christian leadership is not about the exercise of power, it's about humble, sacrificial service.

This was startlingly illustrated to the disciples as they celebrated the Jewish Passover. They were also made to realize that, despite the events that were about to transpire, Jesus was in control! He understood what was going on and wanted to use these final hours with the disciples to prepare them for all that was to come.

Foot-washing for beginners (13:1–17)

They've sat down to the Passover meal—actually, it's more a case of them reclining on their left arms—when their friend, master and teacher gets up, puts on a towel and begins to wash their feet.

Now, this was shocking. This was something so menial that the Jews of the day would not even allow their Jewish servants to do it (they had to get in Gentiles for the job). And you can understand why—sandal-covered feet would pick up all the dirt, dust and manure found on the streets. But Jesus, the one they believed to be God's promised Son and Messiah, bent down to their feet and washed them.

You can sense the shock and puzzlement that all the disciples felt. As usual, it was impetuous Peter who put into words what they were all thinking: 'Lord, are you going to wash my feet?' (v. 6). It didn't make sense. This wasn't how things were done. What did it all actually mean? Peter couldn't possibly allow Jesus to wash his feet; it just didn't seem right (vv. 6–9). Jesus made it clear to him that he would later understand the significance of what was being done: 'You do not realise *now* what I am doing, but *later* you will understand.'

In the context of this passage, which begins in verse 1 with 'Jesus knew that the time had come for him to leave this world and go to the Father', it is clear that the 'later' which Jesus referred to was his coming death on the cross. He was telling Peter that he would understand what was being done when he grasped the significance of Calvary. This became even clearer when Jesus went on to tell Peter that 'Unless I wash you, you have no part with me'. What Jesus was picturing here was not the dirt found on the soles of feet but the dirt found in the souls of people. He was talking about the fact that if anyone is to enjoy friendship with God, he or she must be made clean from sin and selfishness, rebellion and failure.

This was certainly an idea that the Jewish disciples would have grasped. It was pictured in their religious ceremonies. The priests had to have ceremonial baths if they were to serve in the temple, and the worshippers themselves had to wash their hands in specially designated basins before bringing their sacrifices. So Jesus's use of washing imagery clearly told Peter that Christ's coming work would deal with the defilement that separated people from God. Little wonder that Peter responded with his usual over-the-top enthusiasm and was so excited about being a friend of Jesus that he wanted to make sure he was fully clean!

Not only did Jesus act out the work he would do on the cross, but he then went on to tell his disciples that this sacrificial, self-giving humility should characterize their service for him (vv. 12–17). A follower of Christ will be willing to follow in obedience. The church is not a theatre for passive entertainment; it is a family for active involvement.

> The church is not a theatre for passive entertainment; it is a family for active involvement.

It is not a comfort blanket for the inadequate; it is a battleground for the involved. Neither must we imagine this is just a call to hardship. Jesus promised his disciples in verse 17, 'Now that you know these things, you will be blessed if you do them.' And 'blessed' literally means truly happy, truly joyful.

Grace for Judas? (13:18–30)

For three years Judas Iscariot was thought to be one of the closest friends and disciples of Jesus Christ. The inner group even trusted him sufficiently to make him their treasurer. So when Jesus announced at their Passover meal that one of them was going to betray him, they hadn't a clue that it was

Judas. You can imagine the tension in the room. Jesus has just washed all their feet, and that is remarkable enough; but this announcement of imminent betrayal stuns them all.

The words of Jesus's announcement are especially vivid, written as they were by the one sitting next to Jesus throughout this episode, the one who humbly describes himself as 'the disciple whom Jesus loved' (v. 23). And John makes it clear that Jesus's declaration had two purposes.

That the disciples might be strengthened

Jesus had been teaching his disciples some vital lessons. He wanted them to grasp who he actually was and that therefore he could be fully trusted. He realized that, when the time came for his betrayal, trial and execution, questions would inevitably arise in the minds of his disciples: 'How could he be God's Son if such bad things could happen to him?'; 'How could he be the one of all knowledge if he allowed a betrayer in our midst?' So he prepared his disciples in advance for what was going to happen (v. 19). He once again used the expression that the Jews associated with the name of Yahweh God—literally saying, 'when it does happen you will believe that I am' ('I am that I am' was the special name for God). In other words, he was preparing them for the difficult times that lay ahead; times that he knew about and which were in the plan of God.

That the betrayer might be challenged

Jesus not only showed great concern for his followers, he also demonstrated amazing mercy towards Judas. If ever there was someone whom Jesus should have given up on, it was Judas. But he didn't. Notice the way Jesus kept showing him love until the very end.

Firstly, there was the fact of sharing a meal together. In Western culture we don't grasp how significant it is for someone in the Middle East to share a meal with another. It's a commitment of trust, a covenant of friendship. Rather than exclude Judas from the proceedings, Jesus invited him to the meal. What love!

Secondly, there were the seating positions. This is not stated explicitly, but we have enough clues to make the following deductions. Remembering that diners reclined, rather than sat, at the meal table (leaning on their left sides so they might eat with their right hands), it would seem that John sat to the right of Jesus and asked Jesus who the betrayer was (vv. 23–25). Jesus then gave a piece of bread to Judas, which suggests that Judas was seated the other side of him (the left-hand side). Now why is this important? Because in the culture of the day, the position of highest honour was at the left hand of the host. In other words, Jesus seated Judas in the privileged position. It was as if Jesus was saying to Judas, 'I want you to be near me; and I want you to understand how much I still value you.'

Thirdly, there was the foot washing. We noted how Jesus performed that remarkably humble act of washing the feet of all the disciples—something that Jews considered too menial even for their servants to perform. Yet Jesus put on the towel, carried the bowl and washed the feet of them all, Judas included. I wonder what thoughts ran through Christ's mind as he washed the feet that would soon run off to betray him? We don't know. Scripture is silent and we would be unwise to conjecture; but we do grasp again the care of Jesus for Judas.

But then, fourthly, there was the incident of giving the piece of bread to Judas (v. 26). Although the NIV translates the original word as 'piece of bread', it is a unique New Testament Greek word that refers to an especially tasty morsel that was given by the host to a special guest as a mark of honour. So here we have another remarkable act of mercy and kindness towards Judas. All the time Jesus was giving opportunity after opportunity for Judas to repent, but Judas would not. His heart was hard. He was not broken by the patience of Christ nor by his many acts of love and mercy (vv. 27–30).

'And it was night'; what a powerful description—a phrase pregnant with John's light and darkness imagery. Out from the light and warmth of Christ's presence into the dark night; and for Judas, ultimately to his lonely suicide, hanging from a rope that would snap and leave his dead body splayed out in a field he had bought with his betrayal money.

Impetuous Peter (13:31–38)

So Judas left the room and went off to arrange the betrayal of Christ. The other disciples weren't aware that was his intention, but Jesus knew that events were now in motion. He knew what it was that lay ahead (vv. 31–32), although the disciples probably didn't fully understand what Jesus was talking about initially. It was only afterwards that they grasped the full significance of what he said. They had assumed that the Messiah was going to get glory through military victories over the occupying Roman forces and that glory would come through the trappings of wealth and power. Instead, just a few hours before his mock trial and cruel execution, Jesus asserted that this was the time when he and God the Father would be glorified. 'Now is the Son of Man glorified and God is glorified in him' (v. 31).

Indeed, the Greek word for 'glorification' that John uses has deliberate echoes of the Hebrew word to do with God revealing his splendour. Some commentators suggest that the disciples would have been reminded of Isaiah 49:3: 'You are my servant, Israel, in whom I will display my splendour.'

> The cross was to become the greatest symbol and demonstration of the glory and wonder of God.

So how was God going to display his splendour? How was Jesus going to be glorified? Amazingly, through the shame of the cross. The cross was to become the greatest symbol and demonstration of the glory and wonder of God. At the cross, God's holiness and justice were revealed as never before. The cross exposed how seriously God regards sin. At the cross, God's mercy and love are also revealed in spectacular colours.

A moment or two later, Jesus told his disciples not only that God would be glorified through his work on the cross, but also that he would be seen and glorified through the actions of his people (vv. 34–35). If there is anything in this lonely and fractured world that speaks of the radical difference that Christ makes, it is to be found in a loving and united community of believers. The standard that should mark out the way Christians relate to one another is none other than that set by Christ himself: 'As I have loved you, so you must love one another.'

Peter, in typical fashion, rushed in to try to clarify what Jesus had said (vv. 36–37). He was full of bravado, full of promises about what he would do for Jesus, full of confidence in his own ability to turn around a situation—even to the extent that he told Jesus he would lay down his life for him. Little wonder that Jesus, as it were, raised an eyebrow at such a promise; the reason he was going to the cross was to lay down *his* life for Peter and other sinners.

Comforting the anxious (14:1–7)

The Jewish national leaders regarded Jesus as a threat. Still, while he was with the disciples, the disciples felt secure. But what Jesus told them at that meal shook them to the core of their being. He told them that one of them was going to betray him. Worst of all, he said that he was going to leave them and that they wouldn't be able to find him. He even told their brave leader Peter that within a few hours he would deny he ever knew his beloved master.

What thoughts must have raced through their minds! They probably feared death for themselves, or at least ejection from Jewish society. What would they do? Where should they go? What about all their dreams and plans for Israel's future? But Jesus addressed those fears. Even as he grappled with his own knowledge of the torture, suffering and death he was to go through in the next few hours, he took time to comfort the troubled disciples. 'Do not let your hearts be troubled. Trust in God; trust also in me' (v. 1).

From the time when they were good Jewish boys, the

disciples had known that Yahweh God was absolutely reliable and sovereign. And so Jesus told them to trust what God was doing and what he was telling them, which, he clearly implied, were one and the same thing. Keep holding on, even when everything seems to make no sense, because it is all part of divine providence.

In fact, the encouragement to the worrying disciples was even more explicit. As they grew anxious over their own fates and over what would happen to Jesus, he told them about the preparations he would make (v. 2). This is Old Testament picture language describing heaven. Jesus was probably drawing on what Ezekiel had said over 600 years earlier, when he pictured God's home as a heavenly temple with many rooms throughout (Ezek. 42). Jesus said that it was only because of his going (his death and resurrection) that he would be able to provide plenty of room for all God's children. He was not saying he had to go to heaven to start the building or refurbishment work—it was already there—but that it would only be through the cross that men and women would ever be qualified to enter the place where God is.

And not just that: Jesus further promised that he would certainly make sure that all his people would get to be in heaven with him (v. 3). He didn't go into a big explanation of what heaven is like. In one sense, that would be quite impossible. Rather he gave an even better explanation of heaven—'I will come back and take you to be *with me.*' Heaven is where Jesus is.

Despite all the information and teaching that Jesus had given the disciples, they still weren't sure what he was talking about. They still thought that God's kingdom would be established by force of arms, by overthrowing governments, by powerful soldiers. So it is not surprising that Thomas asked the question they were all thinking (v. 5). And in response, Thomas heard one of the greatest answers ever given as to how people can be saved (vv. 6–7). This answer ran head-on into some of the major suppositions of the time.

Firstly, Jesus was claiming equality with God. For the Jewish authorities this was tantamount to blasphemy. But, secondly, Christ's claim ran counter to what the religious teachers taught the people. They said that the way to God was through religious observance; Jesus said the way was through him. Indeed, Jesus had already indicated in this Gospel (and it will become even clearer later) that the way to God is through the death he would die on the cross. Faith alone in that gracious work is the way whereby sinners can be made right with God, not religious performance. And, thirdly, Christ claimed an exclusivism to which even Judaism would not stretch. He said, without apology and with total clarity, 'No one comes to the Father except through me.' There's no other way. There's no other path. There's no route to God other than through Christ himself.

- He is not *a* way (one of many options); he is *the* way.
- He does not speak *some truths*, or present some good ideas; he is *the truth*.
- He is not just a powerful influence or great teacher; he is *the life*; the only one who can deal with sin and bring his people to that eternal home in glory.

The Counsellor is promised (14:8–21)

Philip was worried. He, along with the other disciples in that upper room, was feeling discouraged. Jesus had said he was going to leave them; that one of them would betray him; and that even Peter would disown him. But Philip wanted a quick fix. He wanted an experience that would bring to an end all their doubts and problems. So he blurted out, 'Lord, show us the Father and that will be enough for us' (v. 8). How did Jesus respond? He told the disciples that their peace and comfort must be found in God alone, through the person and work of God the Father, God the Son and God the Holy Spirit.

The good news that Jesus brought is that God delights to make himself known; that he does not play hide and seek with us. It was this revelation of God that Jesus was talking about in verses 9–11. He was telling his followers that he was the perfect representation of all that God is. When they looked at Jesus, they perfectly saw the Father in action (see Col. 1:15, 19; Heb. 1:3).

> The good news that Jesus brought is that God delights to make himself known; that he does not play hide and seek with us.

Not only did Jesus die on that cross in the place of sinners and rise again 2,000 years ago, but he also goes on working for their blessing and good today (vv. 12–14). Because Jesus was 'going to the Father' (which we have seen is an expression that refers to his death on the cross), believers would do even 'greater things' than Jesus did. Jesus didn't mean 'greater things' by way of size or scope (although this is true), nor the performance of more spectacular miracles; rather he meant that because we live this side of the cross we are able to speak with far greater clarity of what God has revealed. The 'greater things', therefore, are words and actions that point lost sinners to a glorious Saviour.

In addition, Jesus told his followers that when they asked for things in his name he would grant them (v. 13). Asking for things in the name of Jesus is not a magical formula that will get us whatever we want. Rather, to ask in Jesus's name means asking according to his passion and will. It means to want what Jesus wants. It means that, when our hearts are firmly set on the glory of God, Jesus will delight to bring that about.

Jesus was going to leave his disciples. Yet he promised them that he would send another who would exercise the same role as he did (vv. 15–17). He used two titles to describe the Holy Spirit—'Counsellor' and 'the Spirit of truth'.

Counsellor

There is no equivalent English word to the Greek word *parakletos* that is used here. The word 'counsellor' has problems if we understand it in its most popular form—that of someone who acts like a therapist. But that's not how the word was understood when Jesus used it. It has more of the sense of a legal counsellor (a more common use in the USA than in the UK): someone who acts like an advocate or barrister and who will deal with you, present the case to you, and represent you to others when necessary.

Spirit of truth

Notice the connection. How does an advocate work? It is by use of the facts and by presenting truth. Therefore, as a description of the Holy Spirit's ministry we see one who will come to us and apply truth to our lives. That's how strengthening and encouragement take place: as God's truth is presented to our hearts and minds, as lies are answered and doubts are dealt with. That's the Holy Spirit's ministry. He is not a vague force for good—he is God in action applying the Word to sinful and forgetful people (and at times, that can be very painful).

Real *shalom* (14:22–31)

It's no surprise to discover the anxiety and bewilderment of the disciples. What would happen to them? Would they be killed? Would they be ejected from their communities? And what about all their hopes and dreams—smashed within the space of a few short sentences? So it's also no surprise to discover that the whole of John 14 is a record of what Jesus said to the disciples at that time to bring them comfort. In this section Jesus used four images to help his followers.

A resident guest who comforts the lonely (v. 23)

The word translated 'home' is the same Greek word that is used at the beginning of the chapter when Jesus says, 'In my Father's house are many *rooms*' (v. 2). The picture is developing. Jesus said that through his death and resurrection he was making it possible for his followers to be the permanent guests in his eternal home. But before they got there, the triune God—Father, Son and Holy Spirit—would come and be a resident guest in their lives.

A revealing teacher who conveys the truth (vv. 25–26)

While most of the promises given to the disciples at this meal are applicable for all followers of Jesus Christ at all times, this particular promise was specific to the disciples who were there in that upper room. You can imagine their concerns—how are we going to remember everything he said to us? How can we tell others what he said? Jesus comforted them by telling them that one of the jobs of the Holy Spirit would be to remind them precisely and accurately of everything he had said. That accounts for the remarkable accuracy and consistency of the New Testament record. It was supernatural that various men could naturally and personally record the life and teaching of Jesus and at the same time be entirely consistent with one another.

> Jesus comforted the disciples by telling them that one of the jobs of the Holy Spirit would be to remind them precisely and accurately of everything he had said.

A remarkable legacy which consoles the troubled (v. 27)

Jesus knew he was going to die. It was going to be the culmination of God's glorious plan of salvation. But what was he, a penniless, homeless preacher, going to leave his disciples?

Well, it was a legacy that far exceeded anything Bill Gates will leave to his children: a legacy that satisfies the deepest longings of human nature. Peace! And not peace in the empty way in which the world so often uses the word. It's the peace that comes through knowing that your sins are forgiven and your guilt is removed. It's the peace you have when the ruler of the universe is reigning in your heart, when you know you have that place in heaven prepared by God's grace.

A reigning King who conquers the enemy (vv. 30–31)

The disciples struggled with all the indwelling marks of sin and, at times, its apparent triumph. They needed to be assured that the victory was theirs; that there was hope; that there would be triumph. For there is a powerful enemy—described here by Jesus as the 'prince of this world'. But he had no hold over Jesus. As we discover later, that work of Jesus on a wooden cross outside the city walls of Jerusalem would deal a crushing blow to Satan from which he will never recover. What a comfort this all was for the troubled and anxious disciples! What hope it gave them for those next perplexing hours, and what a challenge Jesus gave them to respond in obedience (v. 23) and delight (v. 28)!

FOR FURTHER STUDY

1. Research the idea of being 'clean' in the Old Testament and how it relates to forgiveness. Start with Leviticus 16:30 and Psalm 51:7.

2. Have a look at Colossians 1:15, 19 and Hebrews 1:3. How do these verses develop the theme of Jesus perfectly revealing God?

3. Work through verses that refer to the Holy Spirit in the books of prophecy in the Old Testament. What did they anticipate that the Spirit would do?

TO THINK ABOUT AND DISCUSS

1. Jesus gives his followers the example of 'foot washing'. What does that mean for you today?

2. When you are troubled by events and circumstances, what is it that should bring you the greatest peace and confidence?

3. Are you conscious of the Holy Spirit helping you? In what ways? What means does he use?

9 Preaching and prayer

(15:1–17:26)

Jesus was spending his last hours before execution with the disciples. At this point, John suggests that there was a break in this training and preparation: a move not only in subject matter but also in location. Issues of relationship dominate these chapters—relationship with God the Father, Son and Holy Spirit, as well as relationship with the world and with one another.

Vine and branches (15:1–8)

J esus wanted his disciples to grasp a distinction that would be absolutely vital for the growth of the early church, and that would continue to separate humankind down through the centuries. He wanted them to realize that not all who claim to be God's people do actually belong to God, and he wanted them to be able to tell the difference.

To help them understand, he used the illustration of a vine. It is quite possible that Jesus spoke these words as the group passed through some of the vineyards that grew around Jerusalem at that time. So perhaps Jesus did stop and point to or handle a vine (v. 1). Immediately we are back into language and imagery that had special significance for the Jew. We have seen this throughout John's Gospel—it is packed full of allusions that need to be understood in a Jewish context. A vine was so much more than just a common sight for the Jews; it had been used as a word picture of God's people in the Old Testament.

Psalm 80:8–9 and Isaiah 5:7, as well as references in Jeremiah, Ezekiel and Hosea, underline this imagery. In most of these places the image was used to describe how Israel had forsaken God and desperately needed pruning. So Jesus comes along and says, in effect, that a person is no longer part of God's people simply by being joined to the nation of Israel; rather a person needs to be joined to him. He is the true vine. And this imagery is developed further in the verses that follow.

'Gardener' isn't the best translation in verse 1; a more literal translation would be 'farmer'. Most of the disciples would have understood the rudiments of viticulture that Jesus described here. Although today we are likely to be ignorant of these things, the disciples knew what needed to be done. Every year the vine branches would be pruned back to allow more growth; suckers and entangling weeds would be removed; and the farmer would also cut out the vine branches that had died and produced no fruit.

The question has to be asked: How can we be fruitful? What do we have to do to be a part of God's family? The answer that Jesus gave is quite different from what many would expect (vv. 4–5). If you want to be a fruit-producing member of God's family, you have to be in Jesus. The emphasis is not upon what you do, it's upon where you are; it's not upon what you show, it's upon whom you know. Of course, that is precisely the truth that the vine conveys. Fruit can only ever come as the branches receive the sap and nourishment from the vine. Part of that spiritual relationship, then, is that not only are we in Christ, but also Christ's words are in us. For those who have faith in Jesus and who know the reality of his life in theirs, there is this remarkable promise that, as his Word works upon their lives, they will want what he wants, their desires will be his desires, and their prayers will be in tune with his will (vv. 7–8). But for those who are not in Christ, there are very solemn words (v. 6).

Ezekiel 15:6–7 contains words written to people facing God's judgement. Jesus was clearly alluding to this vine imagery, which the disciples would have recognized. Those who are not genuine believers, who are dead wood and bear no fruit, will experience the burning wrath of a holy and just God.

Life and love (15:9–17)

The disciples knew that if life-giving sap no longer ran through a branch, that branch was dead. It was fit for nothing, and only suitable for burning in the fire. Jesus took this illustration of vital connection and told the disciples that their spiritual life was dependent upon being connected to him. In verses 4–10 Jesus used the word 'remain' eleven times—it was the main theme of his teaching. He constantly emphasized that the disciples needed to 'remain' in him if they were to have spiritual life, in the same way that a vine branch must remain in intimate, vital, organic connection with the trunk of the vine if it is to live and flourish.

These verses are not the easiest to understand. What we need to do is grasp, firstly, that the main characters involved are God the Father, God the Son and the disciples, and, secondly, that the unifying themes are those of love and obedience.

- The Father loves the Son—'As the Father has loved me ...' (v. 9).
- The Son loves the disciples—'... so have I loved you' (v. 9).
- The disciples are called upon to love one another—'My command is this: Love each other as I have loved you' (v. 12); 'This is my command: Love each other' (v. 17).
- The disciples are to obey the Son—'If you obey my commands, you will remain in my love ...' (v. 10).
- The Son obeys the Father—'... just as I have obeyed my Father's commands and remain in his love' (v. 10).

By extending this imagery of organic, circulatory life we can see that love flows from the Father through the Son to us; and that obedience flows back from us to the Son, and through the Son to the Father. Or, to put it another way, the essential lifeblood that all true Christians share with Jesus is love and obedience. If there's no love for other believers, there's no life. If there's no obedience to the commands of Christ, there's no life. The two go together. They are as vitally and organically essential as arteries and veins, as xylem and phloem, as blood and sap.

These verses reveal the true nature of the obedience and love that should characterize every true believer.

Obedience (v. 10)

The standard for Christian obedience is nothing more than Christ's obedience to God the Father. We should obey the commands of Jesus with the same absolute commitment that he showed towards his Father's commands. The Christian life is not one in which you can exercise a consumer's choice, picking the parts that you find acceptable or pleasing and disregarding those that don't fit in with your lifestyle. Absolute obedience to Christ should be as basic to the spiritual life as blood is to the physical life.

> The Christian life is not one in which you can exercise a consumer's choice.

Love (vv. 12–13)

You can't get much higher than this. Our love for others should be a reflection of Christ's self-giving, sacrificial love that was to take him to the cross at Calvary; a love that didn't count the cost; a love that reached out to the undeserving; a love that did everything necessary to bring the greatest blessing possible to rebels.

An inward experience and an outward expression accompany this life:

The *inward experience* is that of joy (v. 11). There are some who think that to obey the commands of Jesus will be boring; that it will limit our fun. Indeed, that's why they won't fully obey him. They think they know the way to joy better than Jesus does. But what becomes clear is that the perfect obedience of Christ to the will of God the Father ultimately resulted in joy, even on the way of the cross (see Heb. 12:2).

But Jesus also spoke of an *outward expression* (v. 16). This is picking up on what Jesus had said earlier about bearing fruit (vv. 2, 4, 5). So what is this fruit that Jesus is looking for? It is not Christian love. Jesus did not refer to that as fruit. It becomes clear from the expression 'fruit that will last' that this fruit is nothing less than others who come to saving faith through our work and witness.

So the inward experience of being in Christ is joy, and the outward expression is that there will be a passion and concern for men and women who are lost and without Christ. That's the fruit that marks out the genuine believer.

Hatred of the world (15:18–16:4)

As Jesus continued to prepare his disciples for the days ahead he told them that their message would not be welcomed with open arms. Quite the opposite—the world would hate them. When John talks about the 'world', he doesn't mean the created world or humankind; he means godless society. And this hatred was primarily directed at Christ and, through him, to the disciples, because they were intimately connected to Christ. But it was Jesus they hated first and foremost. Why does the world hate Christ? Jesus gives us several reasons.

During his ministry, Jesus repeatedly emphasized that he was speaking God's words. In fact, he claimed that as God the Son he was in a unique and equal position with God the Father. He didn't come just as a new religious teacher, bringing new insights into what previous rabbis had suggested; rather, when he spoke, we read that people were astounded at his authority. And it was that divine authority that aggravated others (15:21, 23–24; 16:3).

Jesus was not saying that people lived in sinless perfection before he came, but rather that, as a result of his words which revealed the true character of God, they could no longer hide behind their own inventions and ideas. They came face to face with the demands of God. There was no longer any place to hide. There was 'no excuse' for their sin (15:22).

It was not only what Jesus said that provoked hatred, it was what he did as well. Just as his words exposed their sin, so did his actions (15:24). They confirmed his authority and underlined his words. And yet, despite this obvious proof, the people remained hardened in their sin and convinced in their hatred.

It is only when we have grasped the depth of the world's hatred of Christ that we can begin to understand why the world hates Christians. It's because Christians have the same effect, proclaim the same message and reveal the same standard. They are the very representatives of all that Jesus is and stands for. As seen from the earlier verses in chapter 15, Christians are so intimately connected and related to Christ that his life is seen in their lives. And therefore they will be hated also (15:18–19).

But out of this severe warning comes good news for the

believer. Such was Christ's care for his disciples that he didn't want this inevitable opposition to take them by surprise. They may have thought that their fellow Jewish citizens would welcome with open arms the news of their Messiah. But their experience was going to be quite different (16:2).

Some have assumed that the work of the Holy Spirit is to testify about Jesus to unbelievers. But that's not what Jesus said here. He said that he would send the Holy Spirit to the disciples, and that the Holy Spirit would then testify, by implication, to *them* about Christ (15:26). In other words, the work of the Spirit is to make Jesus real and precious to Christians. John reminds us that what happened to Jesus foreshadows what all believers must face. We draw comfort from the gracious work of Christ and by remembering his words (15:20–21).

> The work of the Spirit is to make Jesus real and precious to Christians.

Although this had specific application to those first disciples, who were to be the means whereby the good news of Jesus would be spread around the world, it also gives Christians today the pattern they should follow. They have a responsibility to make known what has happened to them. God has chosen to work through believers, and they must be obedient to the command.

The Holy Spirit's work (16:5–33)

We are listening to Christ's final instructions to his close band of followers. These are therefore the most important lessons that he wanted them to grasp. And they centre on the work of the Holy Spirit, the one that Christ was sending as their helper and encourager.

Back in chapter 14 Jesus had promised the Holy Spirit to his disciples, and over the following verses he had explained what the ministry of the Holy Spirit would be. But now Jesus moved that ministry of the Holy Spirit on one further stage. He told the disciples that the Holy Spirit would come to them: 'Unless I go away, the Counsellor will not come to you; but if I go, I will send him to you' (v. 5).

This assurance was then followed immediately by a description of the effects of that indwelling (v. 8). This is not a description of what the Holy Spirit would do apart from believers, but of what believers would do through the Holy Spirit's empowering. Believers were the ones who would 'convict the world of guilt in regard to sin and righteousness and judgment'. And Jesus unpacked each of these three areas.

Firstly, the Holy Spirit convicts through believers 'in regard to sin, because men do not believe in me' (v. 9). All true Holy Spirit-indwelt believers will expose the empty, self-serving, God-rejecting agenda of the world. There should be something about believers centring their lives around the promises of God's mercy and blessing that exposes the emptiness, folly and futility of the world.

Secondly, the Holy Spirit convicts through believers 'in regard to righteousness, because I am going to the Father, where you can see me no longer' (v. 10). Because Jesus was going back to the glory of heaven, his work of exposing sin had now been entrusted through the Holy Spirit to all believers. This 'righteousness' which is to be exposed refers to the ways in which men and women try to make themselves acceptable to God. Therefore, the believers' task is to expose the emptiness of any scheme that is based upon human achievement rather than upon sovereign grace.

Thirdly, the Holy Spirit convicts through believers 'in regard to judgment, because the prince of this world now stands condemned' (v. 11). The father of lies, Satan, the prince of this world, stands condemned by the cross. The lies put forward by the spiritually blind will be exposed for what they really are. The underlying philosophy of this age will be exposed for the flimsy scam it actually is, and the reality of God's sovereign authority will be acknowledged and submitted to. And it is through the Holy Spirit-empowered lives of believers that all these empty, worldly, godless things are exposed in their true light—not so that we might gloat over others, but that they might see their need and come to seek, find and follow such a wonderful Saviour.

Just as Jesus was the perfect expression of the character of God, so the Holy Spirit continues that ministry of making God known. What an encouragement for these disciples! They weren't academics, but here Jesus promised the Holy Spirit's help so that they would be able to understand the plan and purposes of God. This revelation was not a case of subjective feelings and impulses, but was communicated through words, through an objective, shareable message (v. 13). The reference to 'what is yet to come' is probably not primarily to do with events such as the Second Coming, but rather with understanding the cross and resurrection in the light of all that God had previously communicated through the Old Testament.

So believers today, as then, have this immense confidence that they are not subject to powerful personalities or the mystically insightful, but that God in his mercy has given them both his Spirit and his Word. Amid all the lies and changing theories that this world embraces, they have this certain, sure, absolute Word to lead and guide them.

Jesus was going to be arrested, tortured and then executed. The disciples would be left leaderless, the authorities would gloat over their apparent success, and the disciples would know grief (v. 20). But that grief was going to turn to great joy on the first Easter Sunday morning, as they met with the risen Lord Jesus and ate food in his company again. Although that is the primary application of these words, John also intends us to see that, for all those who love the Saviour and keep their eyes fixed on him, whatever situations or circumstances they may be experiencing, great joy is derived from trusting him. We know he is at work. We know he has his sure and certain purposes. That's why the whole imagery of a pregnant woman going through labour is so effective (vv. 21–22). The pain is so quickly forgotten—delight is found in the life of that new child. In the same way, the trials, pains and difficulties of living in this sin-sick world will be forgotten in the light of his presence.

A glorifying prayer (17:1–5)

Philip Melanchthon, co-Reformer with Martin Luther, said

this of John 17: 'There is no voice which has ever been heard, either in heaven or in earth, more exalted, more holy, more fruitful, more sublime, than the prayer offered up by the Son of God himself.'[1] Others have called this chapter the 'Holy of Holies of sacred Scripture'.

Jesus has just celebrated the Passover meal with his disciples and they are now making their way across the Kidron Valley to the olive grove at Gethsemane. But before they arrive, Jesus stops to pray, and the disciples hear the amazing and gracious words that flow from his lips.

It is a prayer in three parts. Firstly, Jesus prays for himself; secondly, he prays for his disciples; and, thirdly, he prays for all believers. Two words dominate—'glorify' and 'glory'—which together occur five times in these opening five verses.

'Glory' is about seeing and understanding God more clearly; being able to grasp more accurately and deeply who he really is. Understanding this means we can enter more deeply into Christ's prayer—a prayer that has three components to it.

It is about past glory (v. 4)

Although Jesus was here referring to all of his earthly ministry, including the death he was to die within the next few hours, this verse does have specific reference to the ways in which Jesus had already revealed more of the character of God through what he said and did. Do you remember how John gave testimony about Jesus at the beginning of the Gospel (1:14)?

John had seen the pure life that Jesus lived; he had heard

the gracious words; he had witnessed the loving care; he had been astounded by the remarkable miracles. All these pointed to the character of God. So it was no surprise that Jesus was able to say that he had brought his heavenly Father glory by what he had already done—for each action and word revealed something more of the true character of Almighty God.

It is about present glory (v. 1)

We have repeatedly seen that, when there was talk about the 'hour' or the 'time', it was to do with Christ's death upon a cross (2:4; 12:23). Therefore, when Jesus said, 'Father, the time has come', it was again about the cross and how that would bring glory to both God the Son and God the Father. Of course, in one sense, this sounds complete nonsense. How could the cross bring a greater revelation of what God is really like? How could torture, spittle, nails and violent death give a clearer understanding of God's character? The wonder is that there is no clearer, sharper, brighter, more focused revelation of God's character than at the cross.

The cross showed the intensity of God's opposition and anger towards all rebellion.

The cross showed how seriously God regards sin. It showed the intensity of God's opposition and anger towards all rebellion. There is no clearer demonstration in the whole history of the universe of the grace and mercy of God. That's why Jesus was able to pray that he and the Father would be glorified through the cross—that they would be seen for who they really are.

But not only was God glorified through the cross as his attributes were seen more clearly, he was also glorified as his purposes were accomplished (v. 2). The cross was no accident; it was the very culmination and climax of God's purposes. The Bible tells us that even before the creation of the world God had determined for his own glory and pleasure to rescue men and women from every people group upon the face of this planet. God was vindicated as he rescued his chosen people. He was glorified.

But there is still more! God was also glorified as his people were saved through that 'cross' work (v. 3). How astounding! How stunningly gracious! Not only did Christ's work on the cross rescue his people, it also gave them an eternal life of intimate fellowship with the triune God—the word 'know' that Jesus used here was a word that conveyed knowledge of the deepest and most intimate manner.

It is about future glory (v. 5)

Before coming to this world of ours and sharing our humanity, Jesus fully experienced the glory that was his by right as God's eternal Son. But in taking our humanity, that glory was veiled. On the Mount of Transfiguration it peeped through briefly, but when Jesus ascended to his Father forty days after his resurrection, he was once again fully revealed in all his glory. But have you realized that something had changed? When Jesus returned to his Father's presence it was with a glorified body—a body he did not possess before his incarnation. And today, in that glorified body he is as fully revealed as God's one and only precious Son as he was before the world began. Little wonder that John struggles to find appropriate words when he is given a sight of the glorified Saviour in heaven in Revelation 1:12–18.

Praying for disciples (17:6–26)

These are the final words John records for us from Jesus to his disciples at the end of their three-year orientation training. He was preparing them for mission; for the time when he would be gone and they would only have the Holy Spirit and the truth of God. But that would be enough, for within 250 years, their message would have revolutionized all of the known world.

Notice how Jesus made the mission of those eleven disciples absolutely clear (v. 18). And notice that this commissioning was broadened to include all those who would believe (vv. 20–21, 23). So when we have grasped that this prayer is about world mission and the responsibility of each Christian to make Christ known in the world, we can see that it includes the three essential marks of a missional Christian.

There will be obedience to the truth

This theme runs throughout the prayer (vv. 6, 8, 14, 17). Jesus even revealed that the greatest joy comes through hearing and obeying what God says. In verse 13 he spoke about them having 'the full measure' of his joy within, which underlines what he had told them only a few minutes previously (15:10–11). But someone might ask: What does obedience have to do with mission? Why did Jesus stress the need to do what God says when he wanted his disciples to share the good news of grace and mercy? It is because Christians have no right to present any other message of salvation than the one that God has revealed and which comes through faith alone in Christ alone.

To declare that God is the holy Sovereign of the universe and to live in disobedience to his commands is to invite the charge of hypocrisy. Nothing turns people away from the gospel more than the evident double standards of those who declare it. Obedience and mission are inseparable.

Christians are not here to impose their particular cultural brands upon other groups. They are not about telling people what clothes to wear or what music to sing. They are not here to foist their cultural values upon others. They are about the unchanging truths of the gospel which affect sinners and rebels around the world. And the way for any mission to be relevant in any part of the world is for it to be shaped by the principles of God's unchanging Word rather than the shifting values of sin-sick societies.

There will be courage through the truth

There's a problem. The world doesn't want this message. It even hates those who follow Christ. And what's worse is that the world's ruler, Satan, is also ranged against them (vv. 14–15). Once again, this petition would have reminded the disciples of something Jesus had just told them (15:19–20; 16:2). Here's the terrible irony: the people who bring to the world the most glorious and liberating message of grace are the most persecuted religious group in the whole world.

And yet the command remains to go out into all the world and share this life-transforming message. But how can we do it in the face of such vicious and powerful opposition? Again we see the answer in Christ's prayer (vv. 11, 15–17). The answer to persecution from the world is courage in the truth. When Jesus talked about protecting them 'by the power of your name', he was not using some mystical mumbo-jumbo but rather was referring to God's character. That was what was understood by a name—it was the revelation of what a person was really like. God's name meant the full revelation of his character.

So a Christian is protected by resting in all that God is and has promised. We rest in his infinite love; we trust in his infinite wisdom; we believe in his absolute power. So as we go out to face a hostile world, we do so knowing that God is in control, and that he has his glorious purposes which nothing can thwart.

There will be unity in the truth

There has been a lot of debate as to what the unity referred to by Christ (vv. 20–21, 23) really means. There have been global Christian movements which have sought to present a common face to the world. There have been national movements drawing together churches that use the word 'Christian' without any substantial reference to what that means. But that is not the unity that Christ was praying for. It's not about structural unity; it's about an organic unity which is as close and as intimate as that which exists between the members of the triune Godhead—Father, Son and Holy Spirit. It's a unity based upon the apostolic message (v. 20). And that apostolic message was understood to be the essential elements of the gospel. We may disagree with other believers over when and how Christ will return, or over the gifts of the Holy Spirit, or over how much water makes a proper baptism; but as long as we are united in those primary gospel truths, we have the unity that Christ was praying about. Indeed, this prayer was answered at Pentecost, when the Spirit came down and a spiritual unity was established among different groups of new believers.

But it's also a unity based upon the authentic life. Jesus expected that this unity would have the appropriate expression of shared love (v. 23). Christians are different people from different backgrounds with different experiences and different personalities who have been given different gifts and yet are called together into a spiritual family to express their supernatural unity. Where else can such a thing happen? Where else in the world can you find such diversity unified by such love? That's why the Christian family is such an important and remarkable expression of the gospel.

For further study ▶

FOR FURTHER STUDY

1. Starting with Psalm 80:8–9 and Isaiah 5:7, explore the vine imagery in the Old Testament.

2. Read Ezekiel 15:1–8. What do these verses teach about God's judgement?

3. Joy and obedience were linked in the life of Jesus. Explore this theme, starting from Hebrews 12:2.

4. Study Exodus 24:15–17; 33:18–22; 34:5–8; Ezekiel 1:26–28. How are glory and the display of God's character intimately connected in these verses?

TO THINK ABOUT AND DISCUSS

1. What 'fruit' marks out a genuine Christian? How can you show more of this fruit in your life?

2. Have you experienced opposition on account of your Christian profession? How have you coped with this?

3. Christ's prayer suggests that mission is at the heart of being a follower of Jesus. Are you personally involved in that task? Are there ways in which you can be more involved?

10 The arrest and trial

(18:1–19:16)

John selected his material specifically so that we might understand who Jesus really is and what he actually came to do (20:31). It is this particular filter that colours the description concerning the arrest and trial of Jesus.

Arresting the King (18:1–14)

None of the other biographers tell us the name of the valley that Jesus and the disciples crossed—'the Kidron Valley'. But John never includes any unnecessary details; each has significance. As non-Jews living 2,000 years after the event, we could easily miss out on how this detail would have resonated with John's Jewish readers. In their minds, the Kidron Valley was primarily associated with the betrayal of great King David. His own son had rebelled against him and he had to evacuate Jerusalem in a hurry, crossing the Kidron Valley (see 2 Sam. 15:23).

So John is deliberately but subtly helping us make the connection. Just as the Kidron Valley was associated with the betrayal of great King David, so it was associated with the betrayal of David's greater descendant, King Jesus.

Here is another detail unique to John: he records that Jesus took the initiative at his arrest (vv. 3–4). He did not wait for the arresting party to come to him but proactively went out to them. John is again underlining for us that Jesus was not the victim of cruel circumstances but the active participant in God's plan. He was not a slave to fortune but the King of history.

> Jesus was not the victim of cruel circumstances but the active participant in God's plan. He was not a slave to fortune but the King of history.

There is another detail unique to John which we have already noted earlier in this Gospel. When Jesus said, 'I am he' (v. 5), in the Greek it was just two words—'I am'. We have seen that this was like Jewish code for 'God': one of their favourite titles for God, drawn from the time God introduced himself to Moses. John deliberately records the ambiguous use of this answer, as it is another hint from him as to Christ's real identity.

There are many ideas as to why the crowd who had come to arrest Jesus fell back at his response. Some suggest it was because Judas had briefed them on the power of this man; others suggest it was because of surprise at his answer, or because they had a superstitious fear of magic spells, and so on. But John doesn't tell us, because he wants to emphasize the symbolic nature of what took place. People would bow down or prostrate themselves before a king, and this crowd did the same, albeit unwittingly, before King Jesus. Although they were representatives of the Roman world superpower and the Jewish national leaders, they fell down before Jesus, the King of kings. So John is emphasizing that this Jesus was no ordinary character of history—he was none other than the Son of God, God's own promised rescuer.

As we have seen, a big problem Jesus faced throughout his ministry was that people misunderstood what he came to do. They imposed their own ideas and categories upon him, thinking that God's salvation simply meant that they would be able to live safely in a land that they controlled (see 6:14–15; Mark 8:27–33). So it is not surprising that, when the authorities came to arrest Jesus, Peter drew his sword and attacked one of those who had been sent. That's how he still thought. He couldn't understand Jesus's mission in any terms other than of a militaristic, national deliverance. And it is in response to this that Jesus gave one of the clearest definitions of what he had come to do (vv. 10–11). It certainly was clear for John's Jewish readers. They understood the imagery drawn from the Old Testament and referring to the experience of God's holy anger (see, for example, Ps. 75:8; Isa. 51:17, 22; Jer. 25:15).

So Jesus gave a very clear indicator of what he had come to do—take upon himself the anger of God. Indeed, this is the very heart of the Christian gospel: that it is only through the work of Jesus on the cross, as he took upon himself the anger of God for the sins of others, that rebels and failures can be forgiven and saved.

Contrasting responses under pressure (18:15–27)

This is an eyewitness account. Most commentators are agreed that when John writes about 'another disciple' in verses 15–16, he is referring to himself. He was there. He witnessed what went on. He includes details that other writers omit. For example, he tells us that the fire was a charcoal fire (he uses a special Greek word which the NIV doesn't fully translate). He also gives us accurate historical information about those who held the office of Jewish high priest, which in those days of occupation had the equivalent status of a British prime minister.

He tells us in verse 13 about 'Annas, who was the father-in-law of Caiaphas, the high priest that year'. But in verse 19 he seems to contradict himself, telling us that as Jesus stood before Annas, 'the high priest questioned Jesus about his disciples and his teaching'. How could Annas be the high priest if Caiaphas was?

The answer lies in the fact that Annas had been appointed high priest in AD 6 but was deposed by the Roman governor, Valerius Gratus, nine years later. But to the Jews, the office of high priest was one that you held for life; so although the Romans moved to a system of having a different high priest more or less every year (and Annas managed to have five sons and now a son in-law fill that office), the reality was that they still regarded Annas as the official holder of that title.

But John is more than merely accurate in his account: he is dramatic. He arranges his material to bring out some glaring contrasts and make some vital points. He interleaves his account of the trial of Jesus with two episodes of the trial of Peter. He deliberately shifts the scene back and forth between what was happening with Jesus in the informal courtroom and what was happening with Peter outside in the courtyard. And by doing this he highlights a number of contrasts.

Christ was bound / Peter was free

Compare verses 12–13a with verses 15–16.

Christ was truthful / Peter was evasive

Compare verses 20 and 23 with verse 17.

Christ faced violence / Peter faced a girl

Compare verse 22 with verses 16–17.

Christ showed courage / Peter showed cowardice

Although beaten by some, Jesus still displayed wonderful courage and composure, giving fair and straight answers to all the accusations that rained down upon him, whereas Peter buckled under the casual enquiries of a few uninterested people.

Christ faced injustice / Peter was dealt with fairly

Many commentators make the point that the questioning that Jesus went through at the hands of Annas and Caiaphas was illegal. It went against many of the established rules and regulations for trying a prisoner. It should not have happened at night, it should not have been a private interrogation, and the case should have been proven by the questioning of witnesses not the accused. This explains what Jesus said in verses 21 and 23. Peter was given every opportunity to respond to the simple question of whether or not he was a follower of Christ.

They assumed Christ had a large following / Peter revealed the actual isolation

Verse 19 suggests that the night-time arrest was to avoid the risk of what they thought could be a popular revolt. They'd seen the crowds that had gathered to welcome Jesus into Jerusalem just five days previously and were now terrified that Jesus could lead a mass rebellion which would take away their positions of wealth and prestige. Little wonder they questioned him about his disciples—how many of them there were, how they were organized and at what sign they would rise up in rebellion. If only they knew the reality. All the other disciples had run away, and now the leader of the bunch, Peter, was folding under the questioning of a girl in the courtyard below them. All had deserted him.

Christ had prophesied truly / Peter had promised falsely

Peter's denial culminated in a rooster crowing as the first shafts of morning light streaked the horizon. And when that happened, Peter remembered. And we, the readers of this Gospel, also remember what Jesus had said to Peter back at 13:38. Events proved Jesus true and Peter false. They exposed the reliability of Christ's words and the fallibility of Peter's empty promises.

What a stunning set of contrasts John deliberately gives us!

But we have to ask ourselves the big question: Why does John highlight the terrible weakness of Peter and the wonderful character of Jesus? Why does he expose so obviously the appalling betrayal of the man who was going to become the leading evangelist to the Jews and the dominant character in the early church?

The answer lies in verse 14, immediately preceding the introduction to Peter's betrayal. John is here repeating the statement that Caiaphas had made back at 11:50. This is a theme that runs throughout the Gospel—that the work of Jesus was to die in the place of others. What Caiaphas said was literally true—Jesus would die for his people. And having repeated that phrase here, John goes on to illustrate what that really means. He gives us the story of Peter's weakness, cowardice and betrayal. It's as if he is underlining the fact that Jesus came to die for all failures, rebels, cowards and liars, because he came to die for Peter.

The dramatic trial before Pilate (18:28–19:16)

Jesus, the remarkable teacher from Nazareth, had been arrested. He had gone through a cruel mock trial at the hands of the Jewish religious leaders and then been taken to the palace of Pilate, the Roman governor. And before us three scenes are about to be played out.

To understand them we need to grasp where this was happening. Jesus had been taken across the city to the governor's palace, but the Jewish authorities would not go inside the building. They felt obliged to stay outside in the Colonnade area, for the Mishnah law stated that they would become ceremonially defiled upon entry and would be forbidden to continue participating in the week-long Passover celebrations. So, to accommodate them, Pilate came outside the building and addressed them in the courtyard.

There then followed three scenes: three occasions when Pilate dealt with Jesus inside the building and then came out to address the crowd. On each occasion he brought a different perspective. It is a very dramatic situation that John brings before us. As with all good plays, we need to understand the 'dramatis personae'.

The Jews—deceived by religion

On three occasions John points out the deep irony of the Jews' behaviour.

Religious irony

The Passover was that special Jewish celebration that remembered their deliverance from slavery in Egypt. And for a long time the Jewish nation had anticipated the time when God would send his special deliverer and once again liberate his people. This 'liberator' was closely linked to the Passover lamb. So it was the tradition at Passover to kill and eat a lamb while anticipating God's deliverance. The huge irony here is that in order for the Jews to participate in these celebrations, they were actually conspiring to murder the very one that God had promised and to whom they were supposedly looking forward.

Leadership irony

John has already told us the reason why the Jewish leadership wanted to get rid of Jesus—they thought he would gain such a following that a rebellion would occur and the occupying Roman army would take back direct control of all Jewish affairs (11:47–50). They wanted to keep in with the Romans; they certainly didn't want any rebellions taking place. And it is quite possible that Pilate was aware of their reasoning.

> How richly ironic that their hatred for Jesus prompted the Jewish leaders to request the freedom of someone who had actually been convicted of what they feared Jesus would do!

So when he offered them a choice between Jesus and another prisoner, he chose a prisoner who was a convicted insurrectionist, a rebel, a rabble-rouser. We can detect John's irony in how he records this (18:39–40). How richly ironic that their hatred for Jesus prompted the Jewish leaders to request the freedom of someone who had actually been convicted of what they feared Jesus would do!

National irony

The third irony came when Pilate presented Jesus to them as their king (19:15). '"We have no king but Caesar," the chief priests answered.' Here was the ultimate betrayal of Israel's hopes. Throughout the Old Testament it was recognized that God Almighty was their King and that David and his descendants were but God's representatives (see 1 Sam. 12:12).

But now, rather than submit to the rule of God, the Jewish leaders looked to earthly rulers and powers.

Pilate—deluded by power

Not many clues are found about the life of Pilate. Only a few writers of the time mention him.

It would seem he had been a freed slave from Spain who made his way through the ranks of the Roman legions before meeting and marrying a granddaughter of the Emperor Augustus. As a result of those family links he was appointed to govern the province of Judea just four years before these events.

He wasn't a great administrator and made a number of mistakes—such as parading inflammatory banners near the temple, robbing the temple funds to help build an aqueduct and even attacking and killing a number of Jews while they worshipped. As a result, he had been warned by the authorities in Rome not to incite any more disturbances among the Jews—so this trial with Jesus was about the last thing he wanted.

Ultimately, Pilate chose the course of action that would safeguard his own position, even though it went against what was evidently right and moral. He listened to the crowd and handed Jesus over to be crucified. To him, as that low-born man, what mattered most was to hold on to his elevated position of power and responsibility. The irony here is that such a decision to listen to others rather than God inevitably brings disappointment. It was so for Pilate. Six years after this, a complaint was made against him for the way he dealt with a group of Samaritans. He was recalled to Rome, and then exiled to Gaul, where he committed suicide.

Barabbas—delivered by grace

Of all the characters mentioned in this account, none seems more undeserving than Barabbas. There is nothing to commend him to us. He was an insurrectionist, a murderer, a rabble-rouser. And yet it was Barabbas who found himself walking free. Jesus died in his place. This, of course, is John's recurring theme. We noted this with regard to cowardly Peter.

Imagine how Barabbas felt. He'd been incarcerated in a cell not far away from these proceedings. He wouldn't have been able to hear what Pilate said, but he most likely would have heard the shouts of the crowd: 'Crucify him!'

He must have feared the worst, but he emerged to discover that, for no reason of his own, he was being set free. He was being 'graced', being given something that he didn't deserve. Another was taking his place. And this is the gospel story. This is once again what John is hinting at. People who deserve nothing but God's sentence upon them can know what it is to be set free because another has suffered and died in their place.

Having looked at the cast of characters, we now need to focus on the three distinct scenes that are played out before us. Each scene has significance of its own.

Scene One: The innocent king (18:28–40)

Pilate takes Jesus into his palace for the first time. He has been told of Christ's claim to some sort of authority over the Jewish nation and so asks, 'Are you the king of the Jews?'

(v. 33). For Pilate, the issue is whether Jesus poses a threat to Roman rule in Judea. Is he going to lead a rebellion? What sort of military power does he have?

> Christ identifies that the main characteristic of his kingdom—indeed, its main weapon—is truth.

But Christ makes abundantly clear that, although he is a king, his kingdom is of a completely different nature to that which Pilate has in mind (v. 36). But still Pilate doesn't get it. And so Christ identifies that the main characteristic of his kingdom—indeed, its main weapon—is truth (v. 37). Will Pilate respond to Christ's invitation? Will he be concerned for truth? Will he search out the issues concerned and listen to all Jesus has to say? No—for him it is sufficient that Jesus is no threat to his position or to Roman power. And so he goes back out to the crowd at the end of Scene One with this verdict: 'I find no basis for a charge against him' (18:38). Indeed, this conclusion is repeated twice more by Pilate at 19:4 and 6.

While Pilate had in mind specifically the fact that Jesus was not guilty of any political treason, those familiar with John's approach will readily see the added significance of these conclusions—the fact that Jesus came to die in the place of others and take their punishment upon himself. This was only possible because he had no sins of his own that needed to be dealt with (see Heb. 7:26–27).

Scene Two: The suffering king (19:1–6)

But the crowd will not have it. They want blood. And even

though Pilate tries to get Jesus released through the use of an ancient custom, it is the rebel Barabbas who is chosen and freed. The weakness in Pilate's character is revealed. He doesn't want to upset the crowd and cause a problem for himself, but neither does he want to condemn an innocent man; so he tries another tack. He goes for the sympathy vote. He hopes to satisfy their bloodlust through a thorough beating.

And so Jesus is taken back into the governor's palace and handed over to the soldiers so that they can torture him. Indeed, the best commentary upon what happened at this point can be found in the prophetic words of the Old Testament that described this event in anticipation. Let their simplicity record the horror: 'his appearance was so disfigured beyond that of any man and his form marred beyond human likeness' (Isa. 52:14).

But John doesn't emphasize these things. He doesn't dwell on the brutality and horror of what took place. Rather he has something more important for us to notice. It is the incredible irony that the man so vilely and cruelly beaten is none other than the King (19:2–3).

And so Jesus is brought out a second time and paraded before the crowd. Pilate invites their sympathy: 'Here is the man!' But they are not satisfied. They are committed to his ignominious death upon a wooden cross, and so the chant starts up again: 'Crucify! Crucify!' And so begins Scene Three.

Scene Three: The exclusive king (19:6–16)

We do not know why Pilate 'was even more afraid' when

he heard that Jesus 'claimed to be the Son of God'. He is a hardened soldier, a natural cynic. But there's something different here, something unique about the one standing before him. Has Pilate seen enough to know that these outrageous claims actually have substance to them? That this Jesus is actually divine?

We just don't know. We're not told. But what follows reveals that the issue at stake is one of authority—who really is in control? Jesus turns the tables on Pilate. It's as if Pilate becomes the one on trial (vv. 10–11). But Pilate is not free. He is fearful of losing his position of power. He is afraid that he will be reported as one who can no longer be trusted as Caesar's friend. Faced with freeing this innocent man or bowing to the veiled threats of the Jewish authorities, he capitulates and hands Jesus over for execution (vv. 12–16).

But just as Pilate will not recognize the rule and authority of Jesus, preferring instead the temporary trappings of wealth and power, so also the Jewish authorities refuse to acknowledge the authority of Jesus. It is far more convenient to have Jesus removed from the scene and out of their lives (vv. 14–16). Political compromise and national betrayal are considered to be reasonable prices to pay to avoid recognizing the kingly claims of Christ.

FOR FURTHER STUDY

1. Explore the imagery of the cup of God's anger—see Psalm 75:8; Isaiah 51:17, 22; Jeremiah 25:15.

2. What exactly would Barabbas have heard? Look at the shouts recorded in Matthew 27:20–25.

3. Study the evidence regarding the character of Jesus, given by those who knew him best, in 1 John 3:5; 1 Peter 2:22; 2 Corinthians 5:21. What do we learn about Jesus?

TO THINK ABOUT AND DISCUSS

1. How do you react to verses that refer to God's anger? Why is this such an essential part of God's character? Why is it vital that we understand this aspect of his character fully in order to gain a right understanding of the work done on the cross?

2. Why is it so difficult for so many people to accept the fact that Jesus is King? What would be the implications for their lives if they accepted his Kingship?

11 The King is killed

(19:17–42)

The crucifixion of Jesus Christ is the focal point of John's Gospel. Everything has been building up to it. More than that, the crucifixion was the focal point of Christ's ministry. It was what he was deliberately and consciously working towards. This was not the sad postscript to a wonderful life, but rather the very culmination of all he came to do.

Crucified (19:17–27)

Given this, the brevity and simplicity with which John records the event are startling (vv. 17–18). His first readers were familiar with the mechanics of crucifixion, so John didn't need to go into the details of what happened. Neither does he want us to become so taken up with the physical suffering of Christ that we miss the greater significance of what was taking place. But it is appropriate that we should be aware of what lay behind these summary words of John.

Firstly, it seems quite likely that when the soldiers took charge of Christ they would have given him an additional beating to weaken his body prior to crucifixion. The cross beam (*patibulum*) was then placed upon his shoulders and he began to carry it out towards the place of execution, known as 'the place of the Skull', which in the local Aramaic language was translated 'Golgotha' and is known by us today as 'Calvary', the Latin translation of the same expression.

At Calvary the upright beam would already have been in place, so Christ would have been laid on his back and his hands nailed (through the wrists) to the cross piece. This was then raised up and fastened to the upright beam. Nails were then hammered through the feet, which were probably allowed to rest upon a small piece of wood (*sedecula*) that was attached to the upright beam and which partially supported the body's weight. This was there to prolong the agony of death.

It was the cruellest form of execution, intended to provide an indelible warning to all who witnessed the event. On average, it took a victim three days to die, although some had been known to last for up to nine. 'It was the most cruel and shameful of all punishments,' said the Roman statesman-philosopher Cicero. 'Let it never come near the body of a Roman citizen; nay, not even near his thoughts or eyes or ears.'[1]

While carrying the cross beam out to the place of execution, it was common for the victim to wear around his neck the record of the crime for which he was being executed. This was then often fastened to the cross where he hung. In yet another act of bitterness against the Jewish authorities Pilate taunted them with the following written charge: 'Jesus of Nazareth, the King of the Jews'. And this was written in three languages: Aramaic (the common language in Palestine), Latin (the official language of the Roman army and government) and Greek (the common language used throughout the Roman world—known and used from Spain to Asia).

Now, although Pilate only ever intended this notice to be a provocation to the troublesome Jewish authorities, John again sees the added significance of these words and draws our attention to them. Throughout his Gospel he has been emphasizing how Christ came to rescue and save men and women regardless of their national, social or moral backgrounds. And John sees these words, written in languages that anyone in the known world could have understood, as symbolic of that open invitation of the Christ to all. He is indeed King, not just of the Jews, but of all who will acknowledge his Lordship and rule.

One of the perks for a Roman soldier on execution duty was the fact that the clothes of a victim became yours by right. This execution squad, like many of its time, was composed of four men, and there were five items of clothing from Jesus that they needed to share: a belt, sandals, head covering, outer robe and an undergarment. And because this last item had been woven in one piece, they decided against tearing it and instead gambled for it (v. 24).

There have been a variety of very imaginative attempts to explain why John mentions this detail. Some people see deep symbolic significance in it. But it is best simply to recognize that John mentions this detail to underline the fact that what was happening was exactly what God had planned should happen. This crucifixion, however terrible, was not a mistake. John brings this out by quoting from Psalm 22 (written over 1,000 years previously), 'They divided my garments among them and cast lots for my clothing', and by adding his own comment to underline its significance: 'So this is what the soldiers did.'

John also identifies a number of women who were standing close by to witness the scene. Because of the lack of punctuation in the original Greek there is some confusion as to who and how many were present, but by comparing this with other accounts we can safely say there were four: Mary the mother of Christ; her sister Salome; Mary the wife of Clopas; and Mary Magdalene.

Notice the immense sympathy and understanding that Christ displayed (vv. 25–27). Why did Jesus call his mother 'Dear woman'? It was probably because he wanted to protect her from the attentions of the crowd. To have called her his mother would only have exposed her to the insults and barracking of a hostile mob, but in this way he exercised care for her as her eldest son while protecting her and entrusting her to the writer of this Gospel. It has also been suggested that, by addressing her in this way, he made it clear that their earthly relationship was over. Upon his resurrection she would recognize that she had as much need of his salvation as any other sinner. Her past privileges would count for nothing with regard to her soul. She needed to see him as her Saviour rather than as her son.

The King dies (19:28–30)

Few, if any of us, will fulfil our life's dreams. So much will be
left unsaid, unfinished and unaccomplished. But you could
never use the words 'incomplete' or 'unfinished' for the life
and work of Jesus Christ.

John has already drawn our attention to the fact that,
by gambling for Christ's clothing, the Roman soldiers
were doing just what God had said would happen. And in
this passage we can see how Jesus himself had that same
consciousness of being an integral part of this plan (v. 28).

There is no doubt that a raging thirst afflicts the victims of
crucifixion and that Jesus's statement of thirst was a genuine
response to that. But John is also telling us that Christ was
aware of the prophecies and pictures that had been made
many centuries before, pointing to this particular event (see
Ps. 22:15–18; 69:21).

So we are again reminded that what was taking place on
'Skull Hill' was precisely what God had planned. Jesus knew
it. He had known it all through his earthly ministry.

John doesn't waste words. Every detail is significant.
Therefore we need to stop and ask ourselves why he
specifically tells us that the sponge of wine vinegar was put
on 'a stalk of the hyssop plant'. Matthew and Mark simply
tell us that it was a stick. Luke doesn't even mention it. But
John, having stood by that cross as an eyewitness to these
events, sees particular significance.

We have already seen how he has placed great significance
on the fact that the crucifixion took place in Passover week.
The hyssop plant had a particular link to the Passover—it

was the plant that was used to paint Jewish doorframes with the blood of the Passover lamb, making the mark that meant freedom and safety for God's people. In fact, John underlines this symbolism just seven verses later (v. 36); this was all about the Passover lamb (see Exod. 12:46; Num. 9:12).

On the way to the cross, Jesus had been offered a drink of 'wine mixed with myrrh' (Mark 15:23). It was a form of sedative, something to help dull the pain and agony. But Jesus had refused this, determined instead to drink fully the cup of suffering. Now on the cross he drank the different sort of wine that had been offered him. It was the cheap wine used by the soldiers; something to help with the thirst and moisten the tongue so he could give one loud shout: 'It is finished', which, in the Greek, is just one word: *tetelestai*.

Sadly, our English language can't succinctly capture the sense of this. It wasn't a cry of defeat, of Jesus admitting failure. Rather it carried with it the sense of something being complete and accomplished. The word has already been used back at 17:4: 'I have brought you glory on earth by *completing* the work you gave me to do.'

It was also a technical term that was commonly used in relation to paying tax. Numerous bills and receipts have been found from this period on which had been stamped the word *tetelestai*—'paid for'. Interestingly, tax-collector Matthew uses the term in this way in Matthew 17:24 and Paul uses it in this sense in Romans 13:6. So Christ's cry from the cross could also legitimately be translated as 'It is completely paid'. All that had to be done to rescue sinners had been accomplished.

No one took Christ's life from him. They couldn't. Jesus

No one took Christ's life from him. They couldn't. Jesus himself laid down his life.

himself laid down his life. The words John uses literally mean 'he handed over his spirit' (v. 30). This was the final act of obedience to his heavenly Father. And as we watch this scene unfold with John, we again remember those words heard earlier in his Gospel: 'I am the good shepherd. The good shepherd lays down his life for the sheep' (10:11); 'Greater love has no one than this, that he lay down his life for his friends' (15:13).

The burial (19:31–42)

It was normal practice for the Roman authorities to leave a crucified body hanging on a cross not only until that person had died (which could sometimes take many days) but also after death. As the body decomposed and was eaten by birds, it served as a gruesome warning for all who would pass by. But according to Jewish law, anyone hanged on a cross should not remain there overnight.

So, allowing for these sensibilities, Pilate gave the order to hasten the deaths of the three hanging on Skull Hill, using a practice known as *crurifragium*—smashing the victims' legs with an iron mallet, thus preventing them from pushing up with their legs and gasping in another breath. Death by asphyxiation soon followed.

This was done for the two hanging either side of Jesus. However, when the soldiers came to Jesus, they noted that he was already dead (remember, these were trained Roman soldiers who were well aware of the marks of death). So instead one of them thrust a spear into the side of Jesus, and John records that out of that wound flowed blood and water (v. 34).

Now why does John record this detail? It is immediately obvious that John wants to make it absolutely clear that Jesus most definitely died. Although medical knowledge then was nowhere near as advanced as it is today, it was well known that this flow of blood and water indicated death.

With our knowledge today, two theories are suggested for the presence of the blood and water. One is that the spear pierced the heart of Christ, and that the blood from the heart mingled with the fluid from the pericardial sac; the other is that, more probably, the spear pierced the chest cavity where the bloody fluid had been gathering between the lining of the rib-cage and the lining of the lung. This bloody fluid separates with the clearer serum at the top and the deep red layer at the bottom, and it was this that flowed out through the wound.

So Jesus most definitely died. And this was important for John to emphasize because at the time of writing his history (probably around AD 85) there was a group called the Docetists who denied that Jesus was a real man who had taken on human flesh. They taught that it only appeared that he had died. And it was this heretical group through whom Muhammad was to get his idea of the Christian faith; this is why the Koran teaches that 'they did not kill him, neither did they crucify him; it only seemed to be so' (Sura 4.157).

John also directs us to two fulfilled Scriptures (vv. 36–37). The first of these references—'Not one of his bones will be broken'—looked back to what was said about the Passover lamb and quoted from Exodus 12 and Numbers

9. John wants us to notice that all that was taking place, including the horrendous execution of Jesus, was part of God's plan. But the second reference, from Zechariah 12:10, anticipated the time at the end of history when all people will look on God's shepherd and will mourn what they have done. Some will mourn in recognition of their sin laid upon Jesus; others will mourn for having rejected God's promised rescuer and because of their responsibility in his death (see Zech. 12:9–10; 13:1).

Executed Jewish criminals were normally buried in a common grave-site outside the city, but it would seem that two influential members of the Jewish authorities, Joseph and Nicodemus, used their positions to ask Pilate to release Christ's body into their care (vv. 38–39). From Matthew and Mark's account we gather that Joseph was a rich and prominent member of the ruling Jewish body, and from John's account we have already discovered that Nicodemus was one of the leading Jewish teachers in the land.

And what's more, by doing this they made themselves ceremonially unclean. According to Jewish laws, they could not now celebrate the special Sabbath of the Passover week. By handling a dead body they were now excluded from these celebrations. But they didn't care. And so they obtained the dead body of Jesus, wrapped it in sticky, fragrant spices, and placed it in a new tomb that Joseph had previously prepared for his own burial.

FOR FURTHER STUDY

1. Study the Old Testament references that anticipate the death of Christ (such as Ps. 22:15–18; 69:21; Isa. 53) and see how exactly these prophecies were fulfilled.

2. John is keen to link in the Passover celebrations with the crucifixion. Have a look at Exodus 12:46 and Numbers 9:12. What is the significance of these verses?

TO THINK ABOUT AND DISCUSS

1. Have there been times when you have been conscious of God's leading and protection, even in very difficult circumstances?

2. Why is Christ's cry of completion so important? What does this mean about how we can be made right with God?

3. How would you respond to someone who denied that Jesus really died on the cross? Does this point matter?

12 'My Lord and my God'

(20:1–31)

Everything about the Christian faith stands or falls upon the truth or otherwise of the resurrection of Jesus Christ. There can be nothing more serious or life-changing than the question as to whether Jesus Christ is really alive. Of all the 'signs' recorded throughout this Gospel, none is greater than this. And so John records for us in this chapter comprehensive confirmation of this event, leading to belief and Thomas's glorious conclusion.

The empty tomb (20:1–9)

If the resurrection were a hoax, constructed (for some reason) by the apostles, they would most definitely not have had as their primary eyewitness a woman of dubious moral character. Instead they would have chosen a respected male member of the community, for a woman's evidence, according to the Mishnah, was not normally admissible in court.

And there had certainly been question marks over Mary's character. In Luke 8:2 we read about 'Mary (called Magdalene) from whom seven demons had come out'. And several have suggested that this Mary was the one described as the woman who had lived a sinful life and anointed Jesus's feet with perfume and wept over them (Luke 7:36). If we were constructing this story, we would *not* have chosen Mary. But her presence here strongly underlines that John was recording what actually took place.

Grave-robbing had become such a problem within the Roman Empire that about fifteen years after these events Emperor Claudius declared it a crime punishable by death. Probably the value of the myrrh and aloes (19:39) would have made the body of Christ a valuable commodity. So it is no wonder that, when Mary discovered that the stone had been rolled away from the entrance to the tomb and had seen that the body was gone, she assumed that it had been stolen. This was what she reported back to the disciples Peter and John (v. 2). It is very likely, therefore, that this was what they also assumed had happened, and they ran off to the tomb to investigate. They were not expecting Jesus to rise from the dead; that was far from their thoughts. Despite all the things he had told them, they were not expecting that miraculous event (vv. 3–7). So off they ran to the tomb, the younger John outpacing older Peter.

They had been expecting to see an empty stone bench, or even maybe just a dead body stripped of the valuable linen cloths and even more valuable spices; but what they saw put out of their heads any idea of grave-robbers. Instead, they saw the linen and spices still there in position, but the body was gone (v. 7). It was if it had evaporated through the burial cloths. The linen strips hadn't been unwrapped but the body they were wrapped around had disappeared and they had collapsed on themselves. The same applied to the burial cloth that had been wrapped around the head; it was lying there in its separate position above the main body cloths.

This couldn't have been the work of grave-robbers. No one took a body and left the valuable linen and spices. Nor did anyone have the skill, time or motive to unwrap a dead body and then somehow reposition the linen strips in such a complex way. This was something else.

Eyewitness John wants us to notice the disciples' growing awareness of what had taken place. He does this in a number of ways.

It is revealed in words

John uses three different words to describe how Peter and John viewed this remarkable event.

The first is in verse 5: John '*looked* in'. It's the Greek word *blepei*. The second is in verse 6: Peter '*saw* the strips of linen lying there'. The Greek word is *theorei*. The third is in verse 8: John '*saw* and believed'. The Greek word is *eide*.

That first look of John's was no more than a cursory glance, a brief scanning of the scene. That word *blepei* is simply to do with basic sight. It's used of the healed blind man at 9:7. It may well have been the good Jewish boy's traditional fear of defiling himself by contact with a dead body that kept John from going in and looking more closely.

That next look of Peter's, when he actually went into the tomb, could be translated from the Greek as 'looked attentively'. It's the sort of look that not only sees the scene but also tries to make sense of it. It's used of the Samaritan woman at 4:19.

But the final look recorded by John in these verses carries the meaning of 'perceiving'. It's used at 7:52 and 11:31. The word has the sense of seeing something and understanding as a result of what has been observed.

It is symbolized by light

Light and darkness have been constant themes throughout this Gospel. Darkness has pictured ignorance and sin. Nicodemus came in the night, Judas left in the dark, and so on. But we've also had Jesus declare he is truth and light (8:12; 12:35–36).

John draws our attention to the time when Mary first went to the tomb: 'Early on the first day of the week, *while it was still dark*, Mary Magdalene went to the tomb and saw that the stone had been removed from the entrance.' The sun was just rising. The day started in darkness but was moving into light. That's how it was for those who went to the empty tomb. At first, the darkness of ignorance and unbelief; but as the first light began to seep in over the eastern sky, so darkness began to be dispelled and the knowledge of what God had done became clearer for the disciples.

It culminates in belief

Observe the different reactions of Peter and John. Peter observed the scene closely but didn't know what to make of it. He was fairly sure that grave-robbers were not to blame—and who in their right minds would do it when there were trained Roman soldiers on guard duty? No, that theory didn't fit the facts he'd observed. But what did? As Luke records at 24:12, 'Peter … saw the strips of linen lying by themselves, and he went away, wondering to himself what had happened.' So Peter went away from the scene as an agnostic. Something had happened—of that there was no doubt—but he didn't know what to make of it, so he went away with his questions.

John, however, saw the same facts as Peter but processed them in a different way. As he tried to make sense of it all, he realized that there could only be one answer—this must be of God.

John tells us in verse 9 that the disciples still hadn't worked out that this was the great event that had been promised in the Old Testament, but they had witnessed Jesus at work and had sensed that there was something profoundly significant and purposeful in who he was and what he did.

So John knew. John 'saw and believed' (v. 8). He put together the facts in the only way he could and came to the glorious conclusion that this was nothing less than God at work, fulfilling his purposes to rescue men and women.

Mary meets Jesus (20:10–18)

Peter and John then returned to where they had been staying in Jerusalem. But not Mary. She was the one who had raised the alarm, who thought the body had been stolen, who was broken-hearted and perplexed, and who was now left alone outside the tomb. But the next ten minutes were to change all that and become the most dramatic of her life. They started with her bending down to get a good look into the tomb, hoping to see what it was that had so affected Peter and John.

What grabbed Mary's attention in the tomb was not the deflated grave-clothes but two angels dressed in white. John adds a detail that the other Gospel writers do not mention: that one sat where Jesus's head would have been, and that the other sat where the feet would have been (v. 12). Now this might just be historical detail, but we know John well enough by now to be aware of the fact that by including such details he is also nudging his readers, especially his original Jewish audience, to understand something else.

So what could this mean? What would his Jewish readers have associated with two angels about five to six feet away from each other?

Imagine the traditional flat stone ledge on which the body would have been laid in the tomb. Here was a picture of the ark of the covenant, the gold-covered box that symbolized the place where God met with his people and dealt with their sins. This box had been kept in the Most Holy Place in the temple, behind thick curtains, with two angels positioned at either end, overshadowing what was known as the 'mercy seat', where the high priest presented the annual blood sacrifice for the sins of the people.

Now we must be clear: John doesn't definitely tell us that is what he has in mind; he just gives us the interesting detail of where the angels were positioned. But it is quite possible that he intends his informed readers to make the connection. He wants us to grasp that the death and resurrection of Jesus constituted the final and ultimate sacrifice for sin whereby any of us can come into the presence of God as forgiven sinners.

The angels asked Mary a question: 'why are you crying?' She replied, 'They have taken my Lord away, and I don't know where they have put him.' John then immediately tells us, 'At this, she turned round and saw Jesus standing there, but she did not realise that it was Jesus.' We don't know why she didn't recognize him. It may have been the tears that blurred her vision; it may have been that she simply wasn't expecting to see him there; it may have been that the appearance of Jesus was so different from the last bruised and bloody images of him she had in her mind. But whatever the reason, she thought instead that she was seeing the local gardener and wondered if he knew where the body had been moved to.

His question to her seems obvious enough in the context, but as we listen to it, knowing who was asking, we can detect the added significance: 'Woman, why are you crying? Who is it you are looking for?' And it was when Jesus called her name that there was that sudden electric shock of recognition. In an instant she realized who he was. 'She turned towards him and cried out in Aramaic, "Rabboni!" (which means Teacher).'

It would seem that Mary had probably fallen to her knees in the traditional Jewish form of greeting someone special, and was clinging on to the feet or legs of Jesus. We can understand that emotion. She thought she'd lost him to death, but now he was found and she didn't want to let him go. But Jesus told her to go and tell the disciples of his resurrection.

Throughout John's Gospel, Jesus referred to his

relationship to God in intimate language—he kept calling God his Father. In fact, he did so over 118 times. And this offended the Jews. They couldn't grasp how God could be addressed in such an intimate manner (5:18). But here Jesus told his followers that this relationship of closeness to God was one that had been opened up for them as well (v. 17).

Jesus appears to his disciples (20:19–31)

John records how later that evening the disciples were meeting together. They'd heard the testimony of Mary Magdalene. John and Peter had also confirmed that something inexplicable had taken place. But it is clear that the news had not yet sunk in. The doors were locked; they were afraid that the Jewish authorities, having had Jesus executed, would complete the job by having them killed, too.

But something happened that would change their lives completely and give them a future they never imagined. Jesus appeared. Miraculously locked doors were no obstacle to him. As he stood there and showed them the scars in his hands and side he proved that it was actually him, the one who was crucified and who most evidently had risen from the dead. Things would never be the same again. This was the start of something new.

Christ used the familiar greeting with the disciples: 'Peace be with you!' As with all greetings, its significance could be diluted by overfamiliarity. But John draws our attention to the fact that Jesus deliberately repeated the phrase (v. 21). It was as if he wanted his disciples to recognize the difference that his presence brought to this familiar greeting (see 14:27).

When Jesus appeared to his disciples on that first Easter Sunday, it was not just to comfort their hearts and bring them peace; it was also to lay before them the agenda of the new kingdom. They had work to do (vv. 21–23).

Verses 22–23 have been the subject of much controversy over the years, firstly, for what they say about the Holy Spirit, and, secondly, for what they say concerning apostolic ministry.

It is worth noting that:

- The Greek that is translated 'breathed on them' does not actually contain the expression 'on them'. Rather it simply says Jesus 'breathed' or 'exhaled'.
- Earlier at 14:26 Jesus said the Holy Spirit would be sent by God the Father.
- At 16:7 Jesus told them that the ascension would take place prior to the giving of the Spirit to individuals.
- The subsequent behaviour of the disciples hardly suggests the indwelling of the Holy Spirit. (A week later, the door was still locked, and in Galilee they were toying with the idea of going back to their old jobs.)

It would seem, therefore, that these verses are not about the Spirit's indwelling of believers. The context shows that when Jesus said 'Receive the Holy Spirit', it was related to their future gospel ministry of declaring the gospel. Notice John's connection: 'Again Jesus said, "Peace be with you! As the Father has sent me, I am sending you." *And with that*

he breathed [on them] and said, "Receive the Holy Spirit"'
(vv. 21–22).

This phrase was to do with the promised empowering
they would know when they came to carry out their gospel
work. It was a phrase of comfort, assuring them that, when
the time came for them to be his witnesses, they would not be
on their own. A supernatural work would be assisted by the
supernatural agency of the Holy Spirit.

But what about this work they were going to do? Some
have suggested that verse 23 gives certain individuals the
power and authority to forgive sins. They suggest, for
example, that priests can absolve people of their sins. But
when we understand the tense of the Greek verb we see
what is being said. It is in the future perfect passive, which
means we can more literally translate these words as: 'Whose
sins you forgive shall have already been forgiven them, and
whose sins you do not forgive shall have already not been
forgiven them.' In other words, the disciples did not provide
forgiveness; they proclaimed forgiveness on the basis of the
message of the gospel (see Matt. 18:18).

On the basis of what the Bible teaches we can say to anyone
who is truly trusting in Jesus as Lord and Saviour, 'Your
sins are forgiven'; and to those who are rejecting Christ and
trusting in some other way, we can say with the full authority
of God's Word, 'Your sins are not forgiven.'

The story of 'doubting Thomas' (as he is called) has
inspired a lot of imagination and many guesses. Why wasn't
Thomas present on that first Easter Sunday with the other
disciples? Why didn't he believe them when they told him
about the risen Jesus? What character traits go together to

produce such a man? In one sense, such questions, although interesting, are really missing the point. John is building us towards the climax of his Gospel. This Gospel is all about recognizing who Jesus is: that he is none other than God himself. And John sees that, when we realize who Jesus really is, new life is given. So he concludes chapter 20 by telling us why he has written the whole Gospel (v. 31).

And when we have grasped what John's big picture is, we can then appreciate the role the story of Thomas plays. For three years he had been confronted with the evidence. He had heard the words of Jesus, observed the confirming miracles and witnessed a life that was gloriously unique. And now, having seen the crucifixion and heard the reports of resurrection from reliable and trusted friends, he came face to face with the risen Christ and was challenged with these words: 'Stop doubting and believe' (v. 27).

At this point we reach the pinnacle of the Gospel; Thomas's reaction is precisely the reaction that John wants from all those who read his Gospel: 'My Lord and my God!'

In fact, John makes this absolutely clear by quoting the words of Jesus addressed to people reading this book (v. 29). We may not have seen him with our physical eyes, but with the eyes of faith we have looked to Christ as our Saviour and Lord. We see him for who he is—the Christ, the Son of God, our Saviour and Lord.

FOR FURTHER STUDY

1. Look at Acts 10:36 and Colossians 1:20. How is peace with God directly linked to the work of Christ on the cross?

2. Go through Isaiah 53 and see how many references relate directly to the death and resurrection of Jesus.

TO THINK ABOUT AND DISCUSS

1. What other possible explanations are there to explain why the tomb was empty? Why does the truth of the resurrection matter so much? (See 1 Cor. 15:12–19.)

2. Jesus described God as 'Father' to Mary. Why is this such an incredible description? How does knowing God as our Father affect our lives?

3. Thomas believed having seen the evidence. To what would you point someone if you wanted to encourage faith in Jesus?

13 There's work to do

(21:1–25)

John has reached the climax of his Gospel with Thomas's declaration of faith, but he doesn't finish there. Unanswered questions have been left hanging. There are issues that need to be resolved. And so we have this final chapter, which shows how the disciples responded to the risen Jesus Christ and prepared for their life's work.

Closure on the past (21:1–14)

Although this chapter is an authentic and integral part of the whole Gospel, John's approach is slightly different compared with earlier chapters. For one thing, he seems to assume that some of his readers will be familiar with the other Gospel accounts written by Matthew, Mark and Luke that were circulating at that time. For example, he doesn't explain why the disciples went to Galilee; he just tells us that they did (v. 1). It is only in Matthew and Mark that we are told the reason why they went there (Matt. 28:10; Mark 16:7). And John's sudden change of scene from Jerusalem in the south to Galilee in the north seems to assume additional knowledge on the part of his readers. Not only that, but it would appear that John expects some of his readers to notice the connection between what happened when the disciples were first called to follow Jesus and what is happening here. John doesn't record this, but Luke does (notice the similarities between this passage and Luke 5:4–11).

Of course, it is not essential to the understanding of this Gospel that we know these details. It stands complete on its own. But once again, John gives hints and pointers that will be accessible to the more informed reader. So what is this all about?

The disciples had been told to go north to Galilee (Matt. 28:10; Mark 16:7), but what were they going to do there? And why did Jesus tell them to return to their home roots? They went back to their old trade. They were fishermen. The boat they used was probably one connected with the family of either Peter and Andrew or James and John. And they were comfortable with fishing; they were skilled at it. So while they were waiting, they thought they might as well use their time efficiently and catch some food to support themselves. But for all their skill, experience and hard work, they didn't catch a thing, until a stranger's voice came echoing from 100 metres away, back on shore, asking how they were getting on and suggesting that they tried letting the net down on the starboard side. It was when that produced an immense catch

> Jesus was calling his disciples to move beyond the comfortable and secure life they knew into bold faith and confident obedience.

that John grasped who it was and Peter went swimming back to shore.

Now, why did this happen? I want to suggest that, before the disciples could move forward with God's plan for them to go and declare the good news to all others, they needed to have closure on their old life. Jesus was calling them to move beyond the comfortable and secure life they knew into bold faith and confident obedience. When Jesus asked Peter in verse 15 'do you truly love me more than these?', by 'these' he could well have been referring to the fishing implements that were lying there on the shore, for verse 20 suggests that Jesus was walking away from the breakfasting disciples and was therefore likely to have had in view the boats that dotted the area. In fact, if John is deliberately contrasting this story with that of their original calling, then fishing boats would make most sense (compare Luke 5:11: 'So they pulled their boats up on shore, left everything and followed him').

For Peter and the others there was, no doubt, a great attraction with that which was familiar, comfortable and safe. But Jesus was calling them to a greater work. He was calling them to step into the unknown, to trust him. 'Don't go back' was the message of Jesus to the disciples, and it's still the message of Jesus for those he has called to follow him.

Although chapter 21 acts like an appendix to the book, we must be careful not to detach it from the challenge we saw recorded in chapter 20. On that first Easter Sunday, the risen Jesus Christ had appeared to his disciples and said to them, 'Peace be with you! As the Father has sent me, I am sending you' (20:21). And the following Sunday he had given them a glimpse of what was going to happen: 'blessed are those who have not seen and yet have believed' (20:29).

So it is apparent that they had a task to do. They were being sent out by God to proclaim the good news about Jesus so that others also might believe and receive the new life they were experiencing. How appropriate, therefore, that Jesus should send them back to the place of their first call, not only that they might say goodbye to their past, but also that they might grasp again the task that God had for them.

That breakfast on the beach was memorable for the disciples. As they faced up to the challenge of the future as well as closure with the past, they knew they needed a strength and help beyond their own if they were to succeed. No doubt there was some anxiety and trepidation. So what did Jesus do? He fed them and looked after them. A fire had been built. There was fish cooking and bread warming. And, not only that, the haul of fish was far beyond their wildest expectations—so large that they even counted their catch: 153 in all. And when they checked the nets, they were not even broken! The message was clear; Jesus was telling them, 'I will care for you. I will look after you. I will abundantly supply all your needs.'

And for all those who are anxious about 'not going back', those who are fearful of what it means to take a stand for Jesus, those who are concerned about the cost of commitment, the truth is evident: Jesus is more loving than you could ever imagine, more wise than you could ever conceive and more gracious than you could ever hope for.

Lessons for the future (21:15–25)

It really is amazing to see the people Jesus chose to do this task; they were a motley crew of nobodies, and when we look at one of their leaders, Peter, we find the most unlikely character of all: headstrong, rash, given to great declarations of loyalty and terrible displays of cowardice. And, amazingly, we discover Jesus reinstating Peter to leadership of his kingdom.

Do you notice what Jesus asks Peter about? He's not looking for an apology, nor for a commitment that Peter won't be so silly again; rather he talks about their relationship and asks Peter if he loves him (vv. 15–17). And we need to understand that, above everything else, it's love for Jesus that God blesses.

In New Testament Greek, there are a number of different words used for love, and two of those words are used in the question-and-answer exchange between Jesus and Peter:

When they had finished eating, Jesus said to Simon Peter, 'Simon son of John, do you truly love [*agapao*] me more than these?' 'Yes, Lord,' he said, 'you know that I love [*phileo*] you.' Jesus said, 'Feed my lambs.' Again Jesus said, 'Simon son of John, do you truly love [*agapao*] me?' He answered, 'Yes, Lord, you know that I love [*phileo*] you.' Jesus said, 'Take care of my sheep.' The third time he said to him, 'Simon son of John, do you love [*phileo*] me?' Peter was hurt because Jesus asked him the third time, 'Do you love [*phileo*] me?' He

said, 'Lord, you know all things; you know that I love [*phileo*]
you.' Jesus said, 'Feed my sheep ...'

Now some commentators have argued that these 'love'
words are synonyms and have been used interchangeably
within this Gospel. Therefore we should not read any
particular significance into this interplay of words.

The difficulty is, of course, that the interplay is so noted
and obvious, and that Peter himself reacts to Jesus changing
from *agapao* to *phileo* in his questions (v. 17b). So it would
seem that John intends something here.

When John uses the word *agapao* (as he does thirty-seven
times in the Gospel and thirty-one times in his letters—
virtually half of all its appearances in the New Testament),
it usually conveys the sense of a strong love that originates
from God. For example, 1 John 4:7–8 says, 'Dear friends, let
us love one another, for love comes from God. Everyone who
loves has been born of God and knows God. Whoever does
not love does not know God, because God is love.' Every one
of the five occurrences of 'love' there is *agapao*.

However, when John uses the word *phileo* (as he does
thirteen times in the Gospel—just over half of all its
appearances in the New Testament), it usually conveys a
love that is more of human origin and nature than divine.
For example, John 15:19 says, 'If you belonged to the world,
it would love [*phileo*] you as its own.' John 11:3 says, 'So the
sisters sent word to Jesus, "Lord, the one you love [*phileo*] is
sick."'

I suggest that Jesus is intentionally pushing Peter to see
whether Peter has changed from the brash fellow who made
great declarations of love but was never able to carry them

through, into a man who, because of the bitterness of his betrayal, has a far more realistic understanding of his own nature. He isn't going to rush into great declarations of love (as he did in the past), but would rather express himself with hesitation and care.

'Peter, do you love me with an *agapao* love?'

'Well, Lord, I'm not sure I would be absolutely true to this weak and changeable heart if I told you that, but I can tell you this for sure—I *phileo* love you.'

And this, I believe, was precisely the point that Jesus wanted Peter to reach: a point where he recognized the weaknesses of his own character and yet was absolutely real before God.

This is precisely the point that Jesus wants all his followers to reach: a point of realism and honesty. If we are to be useful in his kingdom, we need to lean completely upon him and feel safe and secure in his unconditional love.

> Alongside a relationship of love comes the responsibility of service.

Alongside a relationship of love comes the responsibility of service. Jesus didn't ask Peter if he loved sheep, he just asked if he loved him. As a fisherman, it is quite likely that looking after sheep was not something that would immediately have grabbed Peter's attention. 'Fishing for people' would have done so, but not looking after sheep.

Of course, in some ways, these words were particular to Peter. He had an especial and foundational ministry to exercise that will never be repeated. But the principle remains for each one of Christ's followers: we are called to serve Christ's people because they are just that—Christ's people, Christ's flock, Christ's redeemed.

If you wanted to recruit someone to your cause, do you think you would have gone about it in the way that Jesus did (vv. 18–19)? Surely you would emphasize all the positive benefits. Instead, Jesus tells Peter he will grow old, helpless and weak, and that his life will end with him being executed.

Why did Jesus take this approach? Because he wanted Peter to follow him whatever the cost, whatever the future might hold. Jesus was indicating that being a genuine disciple costs you everything. Jesus was claiming Peter's life completely, for the description he gave of Peter's future was very clear. Indeed, by the time John came to write this Gospel, that event would have happened: Peter was dead, crucified, according to custom in Rome, under the reign of Emperor Nero.

But also notice how Jesus needed to make even clearer to Peter what true, unreserved loyalty to him really means (vv. 20–22). Jesus was saying to Peter, 'Don't worry about others and what they're doing—your responsibility is to follow me.'

The disciple to whom Peter referred was none other than John himself, the writer of this Gospel. And John uses this opportunity to dispel the rumours that were circulating round the young church of that time that Christ would return before he died. John wanted to clarify the words Jesus used and the context in which they were employed (v. 23).

John's passion was to share the good news about Jesus. He wanted others to know the historical facts and what they meant. And so, as he closed, he confirmed again the trustworthiness of his account: 'This is the disciple who testifies to these and who wrote them down. We know that his testimony is true' (v. 24).

Yes, says John, I have witnessed these things. And there are not the words to describe his worth, let alone the space to contain all the books that could describe the wonder of such a Saviour.

To God alone be the glory.

FOR FURTHER STUDY

1. Look again at Luke 5:4–11. What are the similarities between the initial call of the disciples and their recommissioning in John 21:1–14?

2. Research where, how and why the theme of 'feeding' occurs throughout this Gospel.

TO THINK ABOUT AND DISCUSS

1. Think back to when you became a follower of Jesus. Did you need 'closure' on anything? How did the Lord show you and enable you to deal with it? Are there still things in your life you should be leaving behind?

2. Sometimes we allow our response of obedience to Jesus to be shaped by what we see other believers doing. What are the dangers in this?

3. How costly is your obedience to Jesus? Are there things that you are not prepared to do for Jesus? If so, what should you do about them?

Endnotes

Chapter 2

1 See NIV footnote. Most modern scholars agree that Christ's words end at verse 15.

2 Quoted at: higherpraise.com/illustrations/preaching.htm.

3 Quoted at: higherpraise.com/illustrations/preaching.htm.

Chapter 9

1 Quoted in Arthur W. Pink, *Exposition of the Gospel of John*, vol. iii (Grand Rapids, MI: Zondervan, 1974), p. 90.

Chapter 11

1 Quoted in Warren Wiersbe, *The Bible Exposition Commentary* (Wheaton, IL: Victor Books, 1996), p. 382.

Further reading

Carson, D. A, *The Gospel According to John* (Leicester: Inter-Varsity Press, 1991)

Carson, D. A, *New Bible Commentary: 21st Century Edition* (4th edn; Leicester: Inter-Varsity Press, 1994)

Hendriksen, William, *John* (London: Banner of Truth, 1959)

Henry, Matthew, *Matthew Henry's Commentary on the Whole Bible: Complete and Unabridged in One Volume.* (Peabody, MA: Hendrickson, 1996)

Hughes, R. Kent, *John: That You May Believe* (Wheaton, IL: Crossway, 1999)

Hughes, Robert B., *Tyndale Concise Bible Commentary* (Wheaton, IL: Tyndale House, 2001)

Hutchenson, George, *John* (London: Banner of Truth, 1972)

Johnston, Mark, *Let's Study John* (Edinburgh: Banner of Truth, 2003)

Keddie, Gordon J., *John* (Darlington: Evangelical Press, 2001)

Lucas, Dick, *Teaching John* (Fearn: Christian Focus, 2002)

MacArthur, John Jr, *The MacArthur Study Bible* (Nashville, TN: Word, 1997)

Morris, Leon, *The Gospel According to John* (Grand Rapids, MI: Eerdmans, 1995)

Peterson, Robert A., *Getting to Know John's Gospel* (Phillipsburg, NJ: Presbyterian and Reformed, 1973)

Richards, Larry, *The Teacher's Commentary* (Wheaton, IL: Victor Books, 1987)

St Helen's Church, Bishopsgate, *John's Gospel* (London: Marshall Pickering, 1999)

Vincent, Marvin Richardson, *Word Studies in the New Testament* (Bellingham, WA: Logos Research Systems, Inc., 2002)

Walvoord, John, *The Bible Knowledge Commentary: An Exposition of the Scriptures* (Wheaton, IL: Victor Books, 1985)

Wiersbe, Warren W., *The Bible Exposition Commentary* (Wheaton, IL: Victor Books, 1996)

Wiersbe, Warren W., *Wiersbe's Expository Outlines on the New Testament* (Wheaton, IL: Victor Books, 1997)

Opening up series

Title	Author	ISBN
Opening up 1 Corinthians	Derek Prime	978–1–84625–004–0
Opening up 1 Thessalonians	Tim Shenton	978–1–84625–031–6
Opening up 1 Timothy	Simon J Robinson	978–1–903087–69–5
Opening up 2 & 3 John	Terence Peter Crosby	978–1–84625–023–1
Opening up 2 Peter	Clive Anderson	978–1–84625–077–4
Opening up 2 Thessalonians	Ian McNaughton	978–1–84625–117–7
Opening up 2 Timothy	Peter Williams	978–1–84625–065–1
Opening up Acts	John-Michael Wong	978–1–84625–193–1
Opening up Amos	Michael Bentley	978–1–84625–041–5
Opening up Colossians & Philemon	Ian McNaughton	978–1–84625–016–3
Opening up Ecclesiastes	Jim Winter	978–1–903087–86–2
Opening up Exodus	Iain D Campbell	978–1–84625–029–3
Opening up Ezekiel's visions	Peter Jeffery	978–1–903087–66–4
Opening up Ezra	Peter Williams	978–1–84625–022–4
Opening up Galatians	David Campbell	978–1–84625–190–0
Opening up Genesis	Kurt Strassner	978–1–84625–159–7
Opening up Haggai	Peter Williams	978–1–84625–144–3
Opening up Hebrews	Philip Hacking	978–1–84625–042–2
Opening up James	Roger Ellsworth	978–1–84625–165–8
Opening up Joel	Michael Bentley	978–1–84625–191–7
Opening up John's Gospel	Andrew Paterson	978–1–84625–194–8

Also available

In the care of the Good Shepherd
Meditations on Psalm 23

IAIN D CAMPBELL

112PP, PAPERBACK

ISBN 978-1-84625-175-7

There is probably no passage of Scripture with which people are more familiar than the twenty-third psalm. The words of the metrical version are among the best loved and most often sung of our Scottish Metrical Psalms. Every statement of the psalm is loaded with meaning and with significance and importance. Enjoy reading through these inspiring meditations on Psalm 23.

'Iain D. Campbell's exposition of Psalm 23 is masterful, both exegetically and pastorally. Reminiscent of the late Douglas MacMillan's work on this psalm, Dr Campbell's adds significantly to our appreciation of the psalm; indeed, under his guidance we are led to behold new vistas of greener pastures and still waters. Sure-footed expository genius of a rare kind.'
DEREK THOMAS, REFORMED THEOLOGICAL SEMINARY, JACKSON, MISSISSIPPI, USA

'The book is written by one who functions as an under-shepherd of the Saviour and who is aware of the spiritual needs and desires of his flock, and this experience is very much to the fore throughout the work. Further, the activities of Jesus are described in such a straightforward devotional manner that makes the book a joy to read. It is a book suitable for the heart as well as for the mind.'
REVD DR MALCOLM MACLEAN, MINISTER, SCALPAY FREE CHURCH OF SCOTLAND

Also available

On wings of prayer
Praying the ACTS way

REGGIE WEEMS

112PP, PAPERBACK

ISBN 978-1-84625-178-8

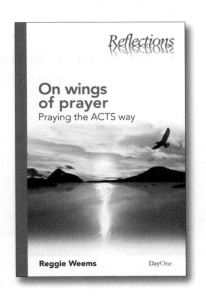

Constructing a prayer life is often like putting a puzzle together without the box's cover. Having a picture makes all the difference. Bible prayers create a model of what prayer can be; exciting, fulfilling and powerful. Using a simple acrostic makes prayer memorable, interesting and focused. You too can learn to pray following this simple outline utilized by men and women who experience the transforming power of prayer.

'This brief work on prayer will encourage you to pray, teach you to pray, and give you precious gems about prayer along the way. It taught me things I did not know, and reminded me of things I had forgotten.'
PAUL DAVID WASHER, HEARTCRY MISSIONARY SOCIETY

'Because of the unique nature of the Christian discipline of prayer, most books on prayer are more inspiring than they are helpful. Pastor Reggie Weems has achieved what only a few have ever done in Christian history. This book is orthodox, penetrating, motivating and inspiring, all in one slender, readable volume. If you are hoping to enhance your walk with the Master, here is one book that will bless your soul.'
PAIGE PATTERSON, PRESIDENT, SOUTHWESTERN BAPTIST THEOLOGICAL SEMINARY, FORT WORTH, TEXAS, USA

Also available

Counsel one another
A theology of personal discipleship

PAUL TAUTGES

192PP, PAPERBACK

ISBN 978-1-84625-142-9

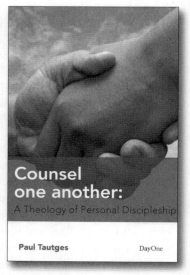

Today, churches are increasingly placing their confidence in Christian psychology as the answer to their need for the ministry of counseling. But counseling is not primarily the work of the professional: it is a crucial way for believers in Christ to demonstrate biblical love toward one another within a gospel-centered, truth-driven, and grace-dispensing church environment. That is the main point of this book.

Solidly rooted in the belief that the Scriptures are sufficient for every soul-related struggle in life, and totally committed to the truth that the Holy Spirit is competent to accomplish the work of sanctification, this paradigm-shifting book will challenge every believer.

In his companion work, *Counsel Your Flock*, Paul concentrated on the role that teaching shepherds have in leading God's people to spiritual maturity by faithfully equipping them for effective ministry. Here he biblically presents, and thoroughly defends, every believer's responsibility to work toward God's goal to conform us to the image of His Son—a goal that will not be reached apart from a targeted form of discipleship, most often referred to as "counseling."

'This book gets it right! Comprehensive and convincing, Counsel One Another shows how true biblical counseling and preaching fit hand-in-glove. Those who preach, teach, or counsel regularly are sure to benefit greatly from this helpful resource.'

JOHN MACARTHUR, PASTOR-TEACHER OF GRACE COMMUNITY CHURCH, SUN VALLEY, CALIFORNIA; AUTHOR; AND BIBLE TEACHER ON THE *GRACE TO YOU* RADIO PROGRAM

'How refreshing—and rare—to see a book like this that asserts the irresistible power of God's Word to develop true discipleship by the sovereign working of His Spirit. This is not a 'trendy book' like so many, blown about by the prevailing evangelical winds. Rather, here is an anchor for authentic ministry that will stimulate real spiritual growth in God's people. May the Lord set an open door before this book and use it to affect the lives of many.'

DR. STEVEN J. LAWSON, SENIOR PASTOR, CHRIST FELLOWSHIP BAPTIST CHURCH, MOBILE, ALABAMA

Also available

Teach them to pray
Cultivating God-dependency in your church

PAUL TAUTGES

128PP, PAPERBACK

ISBN 978-1-84625-196-2

A life of prayer is irrefutable proof of God-dependency. This is true not only of the individual believer, but also of the local church, as evidenced in the New Testament. Churches therefore need to learn how to pray. But who will teach them? In this book, Paul Tautges convinces his readers that teachers and church leaders must not only tell their flocks to pray—they must also teach them how to do it. They must habitually instruct them in the biblical principles, examples, and commands concerning a life of prayer. In short, churches need a biblical theology of prayer. And leaders need a practical tool to help them produce an atmosphere of God-dependency in their churches. *Teach Them to Pray* is that tool.

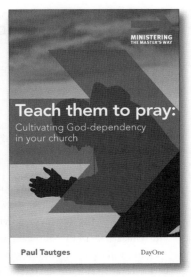

'Paul Tautges not only encourages us to pray corporately, but he also instructs us to pray biblically. This book ... will prove valuable to all members of a congregation. All of us need encouragement and instruction in the discipline of corporate prayer, and this book will help us to that end.'

JERRY BRIDGES, INTERNATIONAL SPEAKER AND BEST-SELLING AUTHOR, *THE PURSUIT OF HOLINESS*

'Use *Teach Them to Pray* as a springboard to cultivate your own ideas on how you, as a pastor or church leader, can cultivate prayer in your church in our day of widespread prayerlessness and spiritual amnesia.'

DR. JOEL R. BEEKE, PRESIDENT, PURITAN REFORMED THEOLOGICAL SEMINARY, GRAND RAPIDS, MICHIGAN, USA

Also available

Comfort those who grieve
Ministering God's grace in times of loss

PAUL TAUTGES

144PP, PAPERBACK

ISBN 978-1-84625-155-9

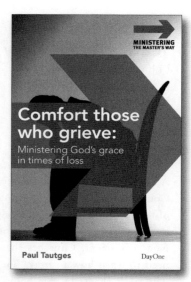

Until the end of time, when the curse of sin is finally removed, suffering will be a large part of the human experience—and a large part of that suffering will be walking through the painful reality of death. Death is not foreign territory that ministers of grace walk upon. As a result, "Death," writes Paul Tautges, "provides a natural opportunity not only for ministry to others, but also for personal growth in ministers." Therefore, church shepherds must not waste these precious and painful occasions that God provides for the demonstration of mercy and the advantage of the gospel.

This book is a treasure chest of pastoral theology that will equip ministers to reach out to those who grieve with the Christ-centered comfort of God rooted in the gospel. The theological foundation espoused here, as well as the numerous practical helps that are included, will help any servant of the Lord to point the hearts and minds of the bereaved to the "man of sorrows" who is "acquainted with grief" (Isa. 53:3).

'Every minister of the gospel will find this book helpful. We are given concrete ideas for consoling those who are dying and then on preparing funeral messages which not only comfort the grieving, but also challenge the lost with a clear gospel message. I know of no book like *Comfort Those Who Grieve*. Most "how to" books are shallow and often devoid of deep theological content. This excellent book is an exception.'

CURTIS C. THOMAS, PASTOR FOR OVER FIFTY YEARS, BIBLE TEACHER, AND AUTHOR OF LIFE IN THE BODY

'Here is biblical, insightful, and practical advice regarding serving those who grieve. Written with the tenderness and understanding of a gentle pastor, this book will be a helpful manual for those who guide others through the valley of the shadow of death. I hope it gains wide distribution!'

DR. LES LOFQUIST, IFCA INTERNATIONAL EXECUTIVE DIRECTOR

Also available

Discipline with care
Applying biblical correction in your church

STEPHEN MCQUOID

96PP, PAPERBACK

ISBN 978-1-84625-152-8

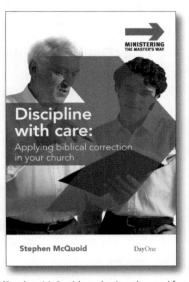

Discipline is one of the most difficult issues in contemporary church life. Church leaders often need to battle to maintain the integrity of their churches, sometimes with tragic results. But why is it so hard? Should we bother with it at all?

In this thorough treatment of the subject, Stephen McQuoid answers these questions and provides a biblical framework for church discipline. Because prevention is better than cure, he shows that discipline is not just about punishing but includes a whole way of life which keeps us spiritually accountable and in a right relationship with God. Corrective discipline will also at times be necessary, and he guides us through the disciplinary stages taught in the New Testament. By using appropriate case studies, he also demonstrates the complications of real-life situations and highlights the lessons that can be learned.

'Stephen McQuoid emphasises the need for leaders not to shirk the correction of members no matter how difficult. In exercising discipline the church is giving God's verdict on the given situation. There must, therefore, be both judgement and compassion. Helpful advice is given to both leaders and members as to what kind of attitude should be displayed towards the offender.'

DAVID CLARKSON, ELDER AT CARTSBRIDGE EVANGELICAL CHURCH AND AUTHOR OF 'LEARNING TO LEAD' COURSE

'In any local church, the issues of authority, discipline and leadership lie close to the surface. Stephen's book explores succinctly some of the cultural issues, scriptural context and practical outworkings of the vital need to keep the body in shape.'

ANDREW LACEY, CHURCH ELDER, MANAGER GLO BOOK SHOP, DIRECTOR OF PARTNERSHIP, SCOTLAND

About Day One:

Day One's threefold commitment:

- To be faithful to the Bible, God's inerrant, infallible Word;
- To be relevant to our modern generation;
- To be excellent in our publication standards.

I continue to be thankful for the publications of Day One. They are biblical; they have sound theology; and they are relative to the issues at hand. The material is condensed and manageable while, at the same time, being complete—a challenging balance to find. We are happy in our ministry to make use of these excellent publications.

JOHN MACARTHUR, PASTOR-TEACHER, GRACE COMMUNITY CHURCH, CALIFORNIA

It is a great encouragement to see Day One making such excellent progress. Their publications are always biblical, accessible and attractively produced, with no compromise on quality. Long may their progress continue and increase!

JOHN BLANCHARD, AUTHOR, EVANGELIST AND APOLOGIST

Visit our website for more information and to request a free catalogue of our books.